"This wonderful book teaches us the language of our soul: how to reconnect to our inner most precious source of power and its relation/connection to the power which created everything. The language is simple and yet so deep—it's a sincere expression of feelings rather than thoughts. This book so skillfully gives us the tools by which we can use this language and become our own therapists, soothing and healing our fears and pains. Moreover, connecting to our divine soul—reminding ourselves about it in the midst of busy sometimes hectic life—creates blissful space, comfort and many times revitalizing our life energy."

—**V.K.,** Yoga Instructor

"This book is an exploration of how to awaken and connect to the divine potential of the soul. Lots of information that was almost read on a soul level. My mind would hear it but my soul was the one who understood it. Was helpful because it provided specific and tangible ways to connect with the purity of my soul. Not too many people can teach that. I feel like this is almost a reference book for the soul. It feels best if I read this in short intervals because the information is so deep that it is almost like reading another language. Similar to *A Course In Miracles.* Almost feels like one could read it through its entirety and then go back and read a page or two daily with contemplations sprinkled in here and there."

—**A.R.,** Ordained Interfaith Minister

"This book is about finding the connection to your inner self and getting instruments to do it every time when you lose it. It is a very easy and understandable way to get peace with yourself. To become aware. Way easier than what I used to use."

—**S.R.,** Dance Instructor

GUIDEBOOK TO THE SOUL: BOOK 1

HOW TO TRUST YOUR INNER VOICE

Uncover Your Hidden Superpower to Live a Life of Peace and Joy

DEBBIE GOTTLIEB, LCSW

A SAVIO REPUBLIC BOOK
An Imprint of Post Hill Press
ISBN: 979-8-88845-342-1
ISBN (eBook): 979-8-88845-343-8

How to Trust Your Inner Voice:
Uncover Your Hidden Superpower to Live a Life of Peace and Joy

Cover Design by Cody Corcoran
Cover Photograph by Dreaming Dee Photography/Deanna Fortier

posthillpress.com
New York • Nashville
Published in the United States of America

1 2 3 4 5 6 7 8 9 10

Thank you, divine consciousness,
for giving me this understanding.

Thank you, reader,
for being open to a new way of living.

TABLE OF CONTENTS

INTRODUCTION

Congratulations, it's a girl!

The first day of my human life began with so much possibility and so much joy. After having two boys, my mother was elated to have a girl. She dressed me in beautiful dresses, took good care of me, and said I was such a happy and curious baby.

We all started as babies. As babies, we had an innate ability to be present, observe the world around us, and try new things.

Do you ever wonder what happened to that vibrant, pure, happy, curious baby? Is she gone, or has she just been covered up?

Let's find out together.

Growing up, I remember being criticized a lot in my childhood home. In fact, it seemed that everything I did was wrong. My mom would kick me out of the kitchen for not being a good helper, for being too slow as I set the table, for not wrapping up the food the right way. My eldest brother would make fun of me, calling me "stupid" when our family was sitting around the table talking and I didn't know about something that happened on the news or couldn't remember the name of a celebrity. I didn't have a voice in my childhood house, so I began to feel small—like I was invisible.

I didn't realize it at the time, but I was slowly losing touch with the core of who I was—my soul, my inner self—whatever name you choose for that part of you that is your essence.

Nevertheless, there was a whole world that lived inside me that was very clear, very sure, very deep, and very wise. I knew things; I was sure of things. But I would question myself and dismiss my ideas and thoughts when they didn't fit with those of the other people around me.

Still, my soul lived on—even though I detached from it consciously and put my attention on trying to fit in, survive, make it, figure myself out, and accomplish things. Why? Because the soul has nothing to do with the body or the mind. It has nothing to do with personality, race, gender, or religion. This part of us is deep. It is pure and untouched by outside forces. It lives inside each and every one of us, awaiting our reconnection with it so that it can provide deeper wisdom and knowing from a neutral and more expansive perspective—one free from judgment, conditioning, and fear.

We are a piece of this life; therefore, when we connect to the deepest part of ourselves—our soul—we are connecting to the life inside us, which is also connected to the life all around us. This connection is such an important piece of wellness, yet it is so often overlooked.

I don't see this understanding as a matter of spiritual belief; for me, this connection is logical. We have been created, just as all life has been created. We are a piece of this puzzle called life, as well as the whole of it. Our mind and our body are the most obvious elements of ourselves. Our soul—because we can't see it—is easy to forget. But it is there, always, much like the air we breathe that we also can't see. Life is composed of the seen and unseen. We must live with both to be fully balanced and complete.

And yet, we don't always do that. We humans like to focus on the seen, so we typically concentrate on the mind and body as we move through this life. Although mindfulness and other tools that increase awareness of the present-moment experience have served to broaden many people's awareness, these approaches make use of the senses and, therefore, still require that the mind and body be utilized. And from what I have seen, they have not fully solved the mental health issues so many people struggle with.

The soul is the key to feeling whole and complete. It is the missing ingredient for total wellness. It is the depth inside of us that is waiting to be reawakened and utilized in our lives. Even if you don't try to utilize it, the soul will show itself at pivotal moments in your life—such as when you get that gut feeling, when things flow for you, and when you just have a hunch about something. The truth is that your soul is always with you, guiding your way. All you need to do is connect to it.

This book is intended to help you do that. From my own life experience and my more than fourteen years working as a psychotherapist with clients, I know that once you make your soul a more integral part of your life, the inner voice it speaks through will assist you in daily living. You can then experience more joy, ease, and peace.

This book is not a book on meditation, breathing, or visualization. This book doesn't tell you to make a to-do list before you start your day. It doesn't teach you to relax your nervous system with breathing techniques, tapping, or affirmations. Rather, it is intended to inspire and guide you to connect to who you really are in real time, instantly. This will feel natural and freeing since your soul is within you, waiting for you to connect to it and live life with it.

In guiding you through this process, I'll first share with you a bit about my personal path—how I lost my own guidance in the course of my Orthodox Jewish upbringing, and then how I refound that guidance through coming to understand the nature of the soul and through the simple practice of being present and choosing to connect. Then, I'll talk about the ways we commonly lose ourselves, exploring the four mind-created universes in which we so often get caught up. I'll offer suggestions for how to get out of those universes in order to return to the soul. Throughout this book, I'll be encouraging you to tune into your body, feel the flow of your energy, and get out of your head. These are key aspects of learning to listen to the guidance of your soul.

This book is steeped in depth and wisdom and will work best if you read it more than once. There will be practices and contemplations throughout this book. The practices are meant to be done in real time, here and now, because that's where the soul resides.

If you do the practices, you will see changes in your life, both obvious and subtle. Most importantly, don't force the practices or the process of learning to connect. Transformation will happen on its own. Connection from your soul must come organically from the inside. That's the beauty of the soul; it flows no matter what is happening.

I hope that my shedding light on this topic helps you to heal from the anxiety, fear, confusion, and discomfort you feel and begin to live a life of peace, ease, and joy.

CHAPTER 1

CHILDHOOD MESSAGING

That baby who loved life and lived in the moment started growing up. No one taught her to connect to her soul, so she lost awareness of this flame inside of her, this wisdom and help that is always available to her.

When I was young, my mother put me down often. "Debbie, you're fat. No one is going to want to marry you," she would say. I remember being screamed at often—mainly for eating too much. Above all, I remember feeling bad about myself.

While much of my mother's emotional abuse took the form of direct messaging, I also received indirect messages from her. "What are the neighbors going to think?" she would say, as though that were the most important perspective in the world. Or, "You can't see yourself the way others see you." This may be true because we all see ourselves from our own lens. But did that mean that my description of myself was dependent on another? That didn't make sense to me.

In fact, little of what she said made sense to me. Something inside knew the feelings she caused in me couldn't be right. That's why I turned to self-help books. I was eight years old when I picked up my first one, called *Feel Good Now*. It helped me recognize that my thoughts created my moods and that if I changed my thoughts to more positive and realistic ones, I would feel better. I did feel better, but only temporarily. In addition to reading, I immersed myself in my religion, did good deeds, and visited places where I felt loved—like my grandmother's house or friends' houses—as often as I could.

I fought my mother's hurtful words, and yet, subconsciously, her abuse still affected me. Fighting didn't actually keep the negative thoughts from penetrating my shell, even though, as she was saying them, I knew they were wrong. And I had support from others that validated different positive truths about me. So, why did all of this still stick to me and cause me harm?

Years later, I would discover that fighting something makes it stronger. Fighting blocks you from feeling. Fighting keeps you from knowing yourself because you're busy with the battle rather than with finding your own truth and living it.

I heard a professional baseball player on a podcast say that he played the sport entirely to prove his dad wrong. He became a successful athlete, but his success didn't provide him with happiness and fulfillment. He was so busy fighting that there was no time for him to uncover his own truth.

Often, fighting becomes a habit you employ in life because it gives you a direction, a purpose, something to attach yourself to. Fighting gives you energy; it makes you feel alive. But fighting is not an act of the soul. Your soul doesn't fight. There is nothing to fight. There is only something to uncover and bloom. If you focus on the other—the person you are in conflict with—you are not blossoming; you are fighting. You may get good results from this, but you will feel empty inside because you have achieved without making a connection to yourself.

If you always come back to yourself, you will always win without a fight because being fully yourself is the best victory there is. But being fully yourself can be difficult when the messages you get growing up condition you unconsciously to think about yourself and the world in a way that may not align with your soul. Messages like this—which we all get from our parents, our communities, and our surroundings—take us deeper and deeper into the recesses of our mind and further and further away from our soul and the truth of who we really are.

While I lived with my mother, I expressed myself, told myself affirmative words, found support elsewhere, and immersed myself in positive activities. Her actions propelled me to do everything I could to help myself be okay. Yet, I still had issues later in life as a result of her messages. How could this be when I was doing all the right things to heal? I later learned that all of the steps I took in response to her actions separated me from my true self. I disconnected from and forgot about my soul. I was too busy trying to survive her emotional abuse by using my mind since that was the only strategy I knew. True healing lives in the core, the soul.

It turned out I was going to have to get back to that place in order to find the happiness I was looking for.

CHAPTER 2

BREAKING OUT OF RELIGIOUS CONDITIONING

When you are immersed in something, there is no way of knowing you are lost. This happened to me.

I grew up in Boro Park, Brooklyn—a sort of ghetto for Jews. I went to a school called Bais Yaakov, an all-girls Orthodox Jewish institution where we were trained to graduate from high school and get married. In our science books, the pages describing reproduction and evolution were torn out.

As a young girl, I believed that religion was important. I would study the Torah with my father and talk to my brother about what was right and wrong, what God wanted, and how I could be a better Jew. I even bought a book on the 613 commandments to see which ones I was keeping and which ones I couldn't keep until Mashiach—the Jewish savior—came. I marked up the whole book in my fifth-grade penmanship and formulated a plan for how to be a better Jew. This felt good to me.

I loved school, had a lot of friends, and was in the school choir. I passed notes and spaced out during class, and, despite hardly studying at all, I managed to average an 88 percent. Life was good. I was happy.

As was expected, all of my friends got married right after high school. I was expected to do the same.

In Orthodox Judaism, you are known as a *kalla mode*, a woman eligible to be a bride, after graduation. You then get set up by a *shatchan*, a matchmaker. The matchmaking process begins when the shatchan calls your parents and tells them about a young man. Your parents call around to find out about him, and, if they get a good report, a meeting date is set. On that day, the guy comes to the house and sits at your living room table where some food has been set—mostly for show. Your parents ask him some questions before you come down, and the four of you sit awkwardly together for a few minutes. At some point, your parents say, "Okay, have a good time," or something like that, indicating that you can leave the house with him. You then typically go to a hotel lounge to talk and drink sodas. If you like each other and want to go out again, you tell the shatchan, who calls your parents, and another date is set. You do this for the first four or five dates before you start talking directly to each other. If all goes well, you're engaged in a couple of months.

I went on at least one hundred of these kinds of dates. All the guys I met were nice, but there weren't any I clicked with or who thought like me. The clincher for me—the day

I decided I couldn't do this anymore—was the day I gave in to my mom, who kept begging me to meet a new shatchan. I finally agreed. When she and my mom and I met at a pizza shop, I discovered she didn't speak English. I excused myself and waited in the car. Once my mother opened the driver's side door, I erupted. "What is the point of this? Is this just so she can see me? I could have just sent her a picture. This is stupid. Enough. I'm done. No more shatchans."

By this time, I was twenty years old. Most of my friends were married, and I was still living with my parents. "What's wrong with me?" I wondered. I questioned and judged myself for not fitting in and not doing what everyone else was doing. But I never thought to question these thoughts or Judaism. This is the way of the mind that I did not understand at the time. The mind takes a situation and tries to make sense of it. If something doesn't fit, the mind keeps trying to make it fit. My mind was trying to make me fit into the world I was living in, the world I was blindly accepting. This created a battle inside me that wouldn't stop. I kept trying to resolve it, but I was trying to do so with my mind. I went into a tailspin of endless questioning—of both myself and my actions. I never once stopped to check in with my soul or explore what other possibilities might exist for me.

This process made me suffer unnecessarily. I became depressed, thinking that there was something wrong with me instead of really looking into my truth and examining what I truly wanted.

We have this idea that suffering—hitting rock bottom— is necessary for change. This is not true! If you are disconnected from your soul and moving too far away from it, this is the only way your soul can get your attention to come back to it. There is a much easier way to create change in your life without ever getting to that low point: You can create change by being connected to your soul and consistently listening to its wisdom. I didn't know this at the time, so my depression and anguish forced me to look inside and start coming back to my soul. I started questioning why I was a religious Jew. Was I practicing out of habit, or was my faith something I deeply believed in?

As I thought about this, I began to realize that religion put me on a sort of automatic behavior plan. I went through the motions of Orthodox practice, but only because I was supposed to. My desire was for something else, although, at the time, I didn't know what it was. Only now do I realize that I was yearning to know my soul. I wanted to find the depth of my being and uncover who I truly was. To connect to my wisdom, I needed the space that comes from silence and looking inward. I had no idea that this was my path; the only thing I knew was that what I was doing was not working for me.

So, I decided to study Judaism in Israel and figure out what I believed. I didn't really get that opportunity growing up because it was a given that I follow the Jewish guidelines and believe what I was taught. I chose the most open-minded religious school I could find there, one called Nishmat in Bayit VeGan, Jerusalem.

There, I met a good friend whose advice changed everything for me. "Debbie," she said, "if you're really exploring, you can't have parameters. You can't only look at Jewish communities, thoughts, and beliefs. Exploring means starting with a clean slate. It means looking at and being open to all possibilities."

Intuitively, I sensed that Orthodox Judaism wasn't for me, but I couldn't force myself to cut the cord. I had to let that advice my friend gave me live and percolate inside me until I was sure.

While I was in Israel, I decided to go on an overnight hike and meditation trip with a group of people I found online. I reached out to the organizer, who told me where to meet at midnight. I arrived at 11:30 p.m. and tried to reach him, but I got no response. At midnight, I had still gotten no response, so I decided to get some food at a place near our meeting spot. The menu was all in Hebrew. In my broken Hebrew, I said, "*Tein le hachi tov bmenu.*" "Give me the best thing on the menu." Out came a juicy cheeseburger. "I guess this is the day I stop being religious," I said to myself. I took a bite of my first cheeseburger—ever. It was absolutely delicious. The chef even came out to see how I liked it; it was clear he had prepared the burger from scratch and put his heart into his cooking. I gave him the thumbs up and continued enjoying my meal until there was not a crumb left. I never did meet up with the hiking group, but I did move toward the next step on my journey of self-discovery.

❋   ❋   ❋

Before I continue, I want to take a moment to reflect on stories. My story may have resonated with you and allowed you to be inspired, to learn a lesson, or to not feel so alone on your journey. Alternatively, my story may not have struck a chord with you at all. It may even have triggered you.

Stories can be incredible teaching tools, but they can also be traps.

I want you to stop and notice how my story may have moved you away from the core of who you are. In all likelihood, you were so focused on the story that you forgot to feel the person reading it—*you*. Remember, connection to your soul is the most important part of everything you do. True change comes from inside.

With that in mind, I encourage you to take a breath, settle back into yourself, and allow your breath to go down into your lower belly until you can feel yourself sitting here reading this book. Then continue.

Remember that no matter how good the story may be, no matter how much it resonates, and no matter how many insights you're getting by reading it, connecting to your soul is the key to lasting change. You know this because, given the number of books you've read and talks you've listened to, you should already be "there." You're not, though, because books and talks and stories are all outside of you. They are of the mind and emotions, not of the soul. They're not bad, but they can move you away from the essence of who you really are.

You must make sure to connect inside as often as possible to awaken your connection to your soul, your true healer and guide.

With that in mind, back to my story…

* * *

I experienced both freedom and profound loneliness when I broke away from my religion. Unfortunately, the loneliness and guilt that enveloped me kept me from being able to appreciate the freedom at first. A strong longing developed in me: I wanted to figure out how to be happy alone. I wanted to keep interacting with others but without needing anything or becoming attached to them. I wanted to enjoy others and enjoy myself at the same time—not an easy task for someone coming from a closed community where the highest value of the group was sticking together. I really had no idea how to move in the world outside of my safe bubble of family and friends. How could I be okay with being myself when doing so contradicted all that I had been taught?

In reality, I wasn't okay with myself at all at this point. I was constantly second-guessing my choices. I hated being left out, and I buried my depression in an overabundance of food. I also did meditations, read books, went to therapy, and spoke with friends. But, although I made some progress, the battle within myself continued for several more years. It continued up until the day I figured out how to connect to my soul and live from there.

CONTEMPLATION: CHECKING IN

How are you coping with a difficult situation in your life?

What self-care and coping skills are you using?

Do you feel like something is missing?

Do you feel like you have a self-care "to-do list" that, in and of itself, becomes exhausting?

CHAPTER 3

THE IMPORTANCE
OF THE UNSEEN

I've always been extremely intuitive. I have a sort of wisdom—not an intellectual "smarts," but an understanding deeper than what can be seen. When I was a kid, I thought of myself as an "old soul" because I knew things I couldn't explain. But I didn't know how to express this wisdom or what to do with it. So, I did what so many of us do with our special parts: I hid them.

We all have this wisdom within ourselves—that part that knows, has a hunch, is in the zone. And yet, we place it in the background of our lives. When it comes out unexpectedly, we say, "Wow, how did that end up working out? How did I know that? It was a miracle, a gift from God!" Actually, that state of knowing is our natural state. All too often, it is concealed by our mind and the reality we see. We live from a place of doubt because we focus on what we see, which is limited, instead of what we know, which is expansive and includes the unseen.

I knew when things felt off and didn't make sense, but I contradicted my truth and discarded my inner wisdom for the collective teaching. So much of my food addiction and inner conflict came from this disconnection from my inner self. It's just so easy to disregard this inner knowing because, in our culture, what we see is what we know and what we can prove. When we're unable to articulate or explain a point we don't have all the facts about, we often feel insecurity and uncertainty. This disconnects us from our soul.

If you really think about it, though, what we don't see encompasses so much of life.

✳   ✳   ✳

Take a look around. Yes, right now. What do you see?

Maybe a table, the floor, the ceiling.

Now, look at one object in the room. Pick something that is standing on its own and can be moved. Now, move it to another location in the same room. Does it look and feel the same as it did when it was in the previous location, or does it look and feel different in this new spot? Move it again. Do this a few more times. Notice that your mind takes things and makes them known and comfortable. By doing so, it tries to make them "fixed." But actually, nothing in the world is fixed; things keep changing, always.

Now, look at the space around the object. Does it change depending on where you put the object? Do you usually pay any attention to the space in between these objects?

The space between actually takes up way more space than the matter itself, but since we can't see it, we often disregard it.

✳   ✳   ✳

I missed so much of life by not knowing the importance of seeing the unseen.

Why should we connect to the unseen, to the soul? What does it give us?

On a practical level, the seen shows us limited reality, and the unseen shows us expansiveness and possibility.

Which would you rather focus on when trying to determine the path of your life?

I had to learn to connect to my soul first and *then* interact with the world.

CHAPTER 4

THE MIND TRAP

When I was young, I was trained to see the facts and prepare for worst-case scenarios. That way, I would have a plan B and wouldn't be too disappointed if plan A didn't work out. At the same time, I thought I was a very positive and solution-focused person because I saw the good in the world. That good wasn't internalized, however. I spoke about what could go wrong and then added in, "Oh, but it could also go right." I was fooling myself. If I really had been a positive person, the negative thought would not have come up. Quickly switching my thought process at the last second didn't make me positive; it helped me trick myself into thinking I was positive. I remained in the never-ending loop of problem/solution and continued to avoid stating my truth directly.

Stating your truth directly—even if it's negative—gives you an authentic starting point. There is immense freedom in stating your truth and staying with it, no matter what other thoughts or emotions show up. It keeps you in the here and now, experiencing the ride of that moment. I believe that the saying, "The truth will set you free," refers to the truth you say to yourself. The depth of life you can experience from being grounded in your truth is unparalleled. It takes you into the core of who you are, and from that place, so much is revealed.

So, why do we not do this all of the time?

For most of us, it wasn't safe to state our truth when we were young. Someone either disregarded it or argued it. It was easier to deny what we thought and felt about a situation than to fight for our truth. This created a split within us where we felt or thought one way and presented ourselves to the world in another way. What created the split? Our mind. Our mind tried to protect us—and perhaps it did, at that time. But now, our mind is standing in the way of our mental and psychological wellness.

Our mind protects us from any situation that feels uncomfortable, any situation we don't understand, and any situation that feels different. It confuses discomfort with danger. "Discomfort" is a broad word that can be replaced by "anxious" or "fearful" or any other word that describes the feeling of something unfamiliar, strange, and tugging. We interpret the emotion we are experiencing as "uncomfortable" instead of just feeling it and getting to know it for what it is. We then get so focused on the fact that we are uncomfortable that we get taken away from the actual emotion itself—the only thing that is actually occurring and the only thing we can actually resolve. Once we get fixated on being uncomfortable and start creating associations around that, we have disconnected from the present moment and become trapped in what I call a *mind-created universe.*

You go deeper into the mind-created universe when you categorize yourself using terms such as "anxious," "depressed," or "bipolar." Psychology has created this language for professionals to communicate with one another. But it has become common for laypeople to apply these labels to themselves. Doing so takes you away from the actual experience you're having. For example, if you wake up feeling down, you may say, "I am depressed." Stating this stops the exploration of what is truly happening in the moment. What may be happening is that you feel heavy, you don't want to get out of bed, or you want time to stop. There is a deeper reason you are having these thoughts and feelings. To uncover that deeper reason, you must be with what is happening in the moment and not in a mind-created universe.

When we're operating from a mind-based place, our soul, which is always grounded in the present moment, cannot help us through the emotions or the event because we aren't connected to it. Instead, we are focused on what is happening in our mind-created universe, swirling around in a never-ending loop of thoughts and feelings, unable to get out of there. This happens so automatically that we often don't realize what's going on. In addition, being in a mind-based universe creates even more thoughts and emotions that spring from the original thought or emotion. The resulting confusion takes us away from knowing what is really bothering us. It's like having a conversation with someone where you are trying to express what is upsetting you, and the other person changes the subject to talk about themselves or something else that is troubling them. When this happens, you cannot resolve what is bothering you because you are straying farther and farther away from what you were trying to work through. We are essentially doing this to ourselves when we go into one of these mind-created universes.

What is the way out? Grounding yourself in the present moment truth. This is your connected place where your soul lives. It will offer you the clarity needed to get you through whatever situation you find yourself in.

PRACTICE: STAYING WITH WHAT IS HAPPENING AT THE TIME IT IS OCCURRING

The next time you find yourself in a "difficult" situation, take a moment.

Notice if you feel what is happening in your body or if you categorize it and go into a web of associations around what is happening.

Can you step away from these thoughts and feel what is happening in your body instead?

Can you stay with the emotion instead of thinking about it?

I have unknowingly gotten lost in a mind-created universe many times. One time that it happened was after I met a guy while waiting in line to get a sub sandwich at my local Publix supermarket. He asked for my number, and soon after, we started dating. In general, I am very picky about who I spend my time with and don't date much. But this guy seemed different; he was sophisticated, smart, funny, and sexy. We had a short but intense relationship that lasted six months. He was all in—or so I thought—and so was I. Then, he left the country and never spoke to me again. At the same time, I was facing financial difficulties and felt anxious about money almost daily. I couldn't imagine how I would be able to navigate all of this, even though I told myself it would all work out.

I was super sad about the breakup. I remember sitting on my couch, thinking, "How could he do this to me?" I beat myself up for falling for him and asked myself all those questions we all know, like: "How could I not see this coming?" and "What's wrong with me?" I went on and on like this in my mind, wasting so much of my precious time and energy in the process. I spoke to my friends, journaled, and listened to podcasts, and yet I couldn't be done talking or thinking about it. I couldn't stand being with myself as these thoughts possessed my entire being. There was a moment when I stopped and thought, "This isn't what I signed up for when I came to this life." I wasn't referring to the situation of being broken up; I was referring to the process of handling difficult situations.

It was then that I realized what was happening: I had constructed a mind-created universe around this event, and there was no way out of it. The way I was handling this issue was taking me deeper and deeper down the rabbit hole rather than getting me out and helping me feel better.

I got this strong feeling inside of me that said, "I don't want to cope with life. I want to live life!"

I had a moment where I just got it. I realized that my soul came into the world to have a human experience and that it would only have come here if it had the ability to navigate life's situations with ease, go after what it wants, and enjoy life.

Therefore, I concluded, *I must know how to do that—no matter what situation I find myself in.*

I understood that the key to life is our connection to our soul. The only obstacle standing in the way of that is our attachment to our mind and the thoughts, assumptions, stories, and reality it sees.

CHAPTER 5

THE WISDOM OF YOUR INTERNAL UNIVERSE

Once I saw the importance of my connection to my soul, I realized that the following statements were true of any moment in my life:

I am either living from my soul, or I am not.

I either recognize I am not living from my soul, or I don't.

If I recognize that I am disconnected from my soul, I can either head back toward it or not.

The *internal universe* is my name for the place where we are connected to our soul.

While connecting to your soul, it's important to realize that you are connecting with more than just *your* soul. You are connecting to the source, the soul of all life. You *are* life; that's why it feels so powerful to be connected to your essence and why returning to your soul offers you freedom and guidance.

Even when we believe in our mind that we are indistinguishable from life itself, we still often feel like separate entities in this world because we are disconnected from the source of who we are. We live life forgetting that everyone—including ourselves—is from this universe, is of this universe, and *is* this universe. This is so powerful to know because it means that our ability to flow with life and to understand it both intuitively and globally is always available. We don't need to look at each piece; we are able to sense the whole and allow it to unfold. This can only occur when you're connected to your internal universe. You have the ability to flow with life, make decisions with clarity, and know what is right even if your mind tells you otherwise. Your internal energy and wisdom become available to you, and your life opens up.

You have certainly recognized that it feels much better and more natural to flow with life and the situations it presents. And you've probably also noticed that human beings do not normally operate this way. Instead, we play and replay situations and possible scenarios over and over again in our mind to prepare for a possible negative outcome or to try to figure out why something did or didn't happen. This is a habit created by the mind. It moves us from one crisis to another in a never-ending loop instead of flowing with life from one magical event to another.

Ponder this: What did we come to this world for, crisis or magic?

While both exist in our lives, we seem to gravitate toward crisis.

I believe every one of us is a soul having a human experience. We are part of a whole and have come into our particular human form for this time of life.

With this understanding, I realized that there are two fundamental realities existing simultaneously:

- We are each a piece of the puzzle of life and are part of the whole.

- We are each a unique puzzle piece playing in life.

Every one of us is a piece of a huge puzzle, and at the same time, every one of us is also a unique piece of the puzzle. When we only focus on our piece, we push and resist. We don't take the time to plug into the overall puzzle of life to listen, get guidance, and flow. I like to imagine myself literally putting my puzzle piece into the puzzle of life and just resting there, waiting and listening.

You must remember that you are both an individual puzzle piece and a part of the big puzzle in order to avoid getting stuck in your story and trapped in your mind. You are so much more than your particular situation. You are so much more than your mind: You are a soul that is made of the universe. If you have the universe in you, then you have universal consciousness and awareness in you as well. You can create and move in different directions. You must remember this ability so that you don't get stuck with your lot in life. Your lot is just a situation in one moment in time. It can—and will—change.

Always remember that the universe inside you will show you the way.

CHAPTER 6

FOUR UNIVERSES THAT DISCONNECT YOU FROM YOUR SOUL

We can only be in one universe at a time. As a result, any movement away from the internal universe, where our soul resides, places us into one of the other universes where we suffer, struggle, and feel uncomfortable. When we move away from our soul, we feel it.

I want to help you identify the four other universes we often end up in—all of which are created by the mind. They are *the external universe, the alternate universe, the should universe, and the others universe*. Being able to recognize them will help you recognize how frequently you live outside of your internal universe. This is crucial to getting back to your soul and finding relief because you first need the awareness that you are not connected to your internal universe to begin the journey back.

THE EXTERNAL UNIVERSE

I recognized that I was stuck in what I call the *external universe* when my focus was on people, places, or events that were outside of myself. I noticed that I was busy saying "them," "he," "she," and "it," in my mind or out loud, which indicated that my attention was directed outward rather than towards myself.

When I was focused on people, I found myself comparing myself to others. I worried about what they thought and what they said or did. I often found myself trying to figure out why they did or didn't do something. I was feeling a certain way because of their words or actions, and I heard myself thinking and talking about them. This probably sounds reasonable; after all, we all do this. However, I recognized that when I was busy focusing on them, him, or her, I failed to focus on myself. I, therefore, couldn't tap into what I wanted, how I felt—not what I felt in reaction to "them," but what I felt and what I wanted from my internal universe.

When my focus was on places, I was worried about what a physical setting would look like and consumed with trying to figure it out. Would it be comfortable? Would it have what I needed? My focus was external, on the place itself, rather than internal, where I could have been checking in to see what I was going to need in that place in order to be comfortable and have my needs met.

When my focus was on events, I couldn't stop thinking about something that was going to happen or something that had happened. For example, if the event was a party, I would be trying to figure out who was going to show up and how to plan all the pieces to make sure it went smoothly. Or I'd find myself thinking about a party that already happened, analyzing what went well and what I wished hadn't happened. I kept replaying it over and over again in my mind.

At first, it was difficult to recognize that I was externally focused and had lost my connection to myself because I was so used to looking outside myself for everything: opinions, solutions, actions, relief. I had done this for my whole life. You probably have too, which is why I call this situation "the predicament of humankind." It started when we were born. We were born with everything we need inside of us—our internal universe—and were curious to explore the world. But we quickly realized that we were dependent on the outside world for our survival. This turned our focus outward. We learned how to manipulate people and situations to get our needs met. We learned what to do to be liked and to fit in. Meanwhile, no one taught us how to stay connected to ourselves while navigating the world. No one explained to us that being focused on the external—on people, places, and events—keeps us from asking the simple internally oriented question, "What do I need?"

You may still be living primarily in the external universe.

Here are some questions that will help you determine whether or not this is true:

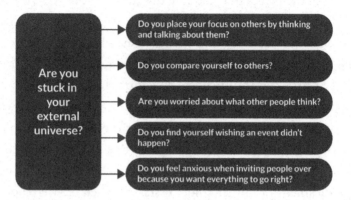

When you hear yourself thinking externally focused thoughts and acting in response to those thoughts, you are no longer in your internal universe. You have left your power center and the home of your solutions.

You can catch yourself being pulled into the external universe by noticing the way you feel. In the external universe, your body feels tense and uneasy. Your energy moves out of your lower belly, your center, and up to your heart/solar plexus or your head. Your thoughts become like a loop that keeps playing and replaying itself. If you can catch yourself by recognizing these signs before you get trapped, you will easily be able to come back to the present moment.

When we're not able to catch ourselves, it's usually because we're attached to the thoughts we're having. We care about the outcome or the event, and we believe that thinking about it and worrying about it somehow helps us come up with a solution. If you believe this, you won't want to change. And, if you don't want to change, you won't be able to create ease in your life on a regular basis.

Situations tend to work themselves out. While they are doing so, you can feel good, or you can feel stressed. Which universe you are in will determine how you feel. In addition, you have the ability to tap into the fullness of life and the wisdom, guidance, and healing power of your soul, which is always available for you in your internal universe. This will help you uncover solutions and live a life that is relaxed and joyful.

If your external thoughts become repetitive because you keep fixating on the external event or person, that's when you know that you got sucked into a mind-created universe. You are now living, reacting, and moving from that reality without realizing you're doing that. The only way out is to leave that universe and enter into your internal universe.

Focusing your attention internally grounds you and allows you to see what your present moment experience is. This makes the external event feel and look totally different. From this perspective, you can ask externally focused questions to try and figure out the details of a situation and to see what you or the situation need at that moment.

We need to look externally in order to interact with the world; however, our focus can be internal during that process.

Here is an example of how to do that. A few years ago, I had to decide whether or not to hire another marketing person. If I did, this person would be the third one since the others did not work out. If I didn't, I would be stuck figuring out how to do marketing on my own, which I really didn't want to do. I discussed my uncertainty about this decision with two people but didn't get any clarity. My indecision popped into my head periodically through the weekend, and had I gotten caught in it, it would have taken me to the universe of thought where my mind would spin the web of associations, what-ifs, and worries. I would have gotten trapped there unknowingly and arrived at the conclusion that I had a huge problem that needed to be solved immediately. I could have let myself be taken away from my actual reality of being in my home getting ready to meet friends. Physically, I would have been in my home getting ready. But mentally, I would have been trapped in my external universe, wondering whether or not I should hire this person—even though, at that moment, I was not going to do anything about it. Since I was aligned and connected and living in my internal universe, I was aware of getting ready and was living in the moment—the only place we can live. In the end, I decided to wait to hire another marketing person.

Your thoughts will always be coming and going. They are part of your present moment experience, much like the movement of air, sounds, and smells. It is only when a thought catches you and traps you that you are taken out of your internal universe and thrust into another one. Once you learn to recognize when this process is happening and become committed to stopping it, you can drop back into the place of soul connection and tune back into your inner wisdom.

THE ALTERNATE UNIVERSE

The *alternate universe* is where the negative thoughts about yourself live. This is the universe where you judge yourself, criticize yourself, and put yourself down. It's where the belief systems about yourself, your abilities, and the world in general are formed. In this universe, you are either revisiting the past or projecting into the future. Your thinking keeps you from being present and from dwelling in your internal universe.

This place was created when you were very young—when you thought or acted differently from the people around you and weren't understood. When you thought you were weird and something was wrong with you, the power of this place got stronger.

Perhaps when you were growing up, you saw a contradiction that didn't feel right to you. You couldn't figure out how to articulate it, even to yourself. Maybe you didn't agree with what you were told to do but were too scared to voice your opinion. After all, no one else seemed to feel that way—or, if they did, they weren't expressing it. You internalized that you must be wrong and that the others must be right. You made up beliefs and came to conclusions to come to terms with these contradictions. In the process, your alternate universe was fortified.

As a child, you almost certainly experienced an event that didn't feel good to you, such as not being invited to a friend's birthday party. As a result of the event, you created beliefs about yourself, such as, "They don't like me," and "I am not wanted." You also created beliefs about them, like, "They are mean," or "I will never play with them again." Your alternate universe reinforced these judgments and beliefs about yourself and the world through the steady chatter of your ruminating thoughts. Today, when you experience anything similar to the rejection you felt when you weren't invited to the party, your alternate universe brings those same beliefs back up again and further convinces you that they are true.

Now, that original judgment or belief may have been true for the experience you went through. But once you make it into an absolute, an "always," that thought sucks you into its world—the alternate universe. A truth in one moment in time becomes a belief system from which you operate. That belief system not only makes you feel bad about yourself and the world, it also perpetuates your negative thoughts. What's worse is that your actions come from these thoughts, further reinforcing them and continuing the cycle. You feel like there is no way out of this loop because there isn't! You cannot get out of this cycle from within your alternate universe, even if you tell yourself that it's not true and try to reason yourself into a better feeling. It's because you are trapped in your mind and moving from your alternate universe. You are not in your internal universe. You are disconnected from your present moment experience and the wisdom of your soul that *knows* that every moment and experience is new and that nothing is absolute.

Trauma can further strengthen your alternate universe. Sometimes we experience an event that is so scary we freeze and can't respond in the way we would have liked to while it was happening. To cope with this distressing situation, we create an alternate universe where we replay the scene over and over again in our mind to try and resolve it, which doesn't work. We might also try and run away from the thoughts and emotions related to the trauma by minimizing it or blaming ourselves for it. This keeps us busy beating ourselves up instead of feeling what happened. Then, when we are going about living our life, the remnants of this event can show up unexpectedly as triggers. When they do, we get sucked into our alternate universe where our mind replays the experience over and over again with no way out. Reacting to the present trigger from the alternate universe that exists in the past keeps us stuck. Often, there is self-judgment associated with the trauma because we couldn't respond in the way we may have wanted to. To make the situation worse, we might not have been able to—and still may not be able to—share our experience with others for fear of what they might think. It is too vulnerable and scary to allow people into our world, so we are forced to process on our own. That processing takes place in our alternate universe, which gets stronger and stronger every time we visit it.

Here are some questions to contemplate to determine if you are living in an alternate universe:

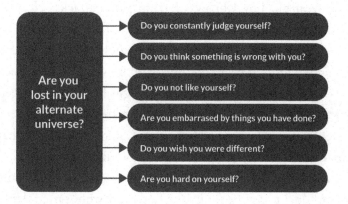

When you start putting yourself down, holding yourself back, and limiting your experiences, your thoughts have become problematic. You are outside of your internal universe but don't know it. You believe what you are thinking about yourself. This universe is very depressing. When you're in it, you feel down on yourself and the world.

If you have ever tried to get out of this universe, you most likely tried using affirmations, such as "I am worthy," "I am good enough," or "I deserve good in my life." They may have worked for the specific situation you were in, but then, when you were faced with a similar situation, you were back in the alternate universe again. This is because saying affirmations without believing them is like trying to convince yourself to think something other than what you are actually thinking. It's futile and continues the alternate universe cycle. You must recognize the fallacy of the alternate universe and leave it.

What makes this universe even more difficult to leave is the fact that we not only believe what it's saying, we also think that believing it is somehow helpful. I once counseled a ten-year-old boy who was having panic attacks. He told me that when he played baseball, he would beat himself up when he missed a ball he thought he should have caught. He would tell himself over and over again how stupid he was for making that mistake because he thought he needed to keep beating up on himself in order to get better. This was his belief system. He was so stuck in his alternate universe that no amount of reasoning could get him out.

All of us find ourselves in the alternate universe at some point—including me. I am a salsa dancer who started dancing later in life. When I'm trying to learn new steps, I sometimes hear myself repeatedly say, "I'll never be able to get it. I'm too fat. I started too late, and I'm not coordinated enough"—you know, all those wonderful put-down comments. At first, they bring me down. Then, I realize that I'm stuck in the alternate universe and that those thoughts are all made up. They are absolute statements that arose from a moment of not getting a move, or from someone making a comment, or from being unable to fit into an outfit. These absolute beliefs are compounded by memories of my past instructor telling me I was too old and too out of shape to dance the way I wanted. The old me would have stressed myself out making a plan for how to lose weight or practice harder. Then, I would get down on myself when nothing changed. There could be no way out through that universe because I was not going to miraculously get thinner or better instantaneously. These days, I still might make a plan—but not from a place of lack. I make it by connecting to my internal universe and seeing how my soul guides me. The only way through is out—meaning, leaving the alternate universe and entering my internal universe where my soul, who will guide me, awaits.

If you are struggling with panic attacks or feelings of anxiety or depression, know that it's not the situation that is causing your feelings; it's the fact that you are stuck in a universe outside of your internal universe. This is good news! Instead of having to change and fix and heal all these different parts of yourself, all you have to do is one thing: Connect to your soul. You will experience instantaneous relief and, as I like to say, "feel neutral or better no matter what the situation is." The rest will be taken care of naturally and gradually in its right time.

THE SHOULD UNIVERSE

Have you ever seen people who seem to have everything but are miserable, depressed, and anxious? Perhaps you are one of them.

These people may be trapped in what I call the *should universe.* They are doing everything they *should* be doing but have not checked in with themselves to see if they *want* to be doing these things. Many of these people have been conditioned to let society determine what their next step *should* be, what their career *should* be, and how they *should* live their lives. Often, these people feel ashamed that they're struggling. They're trying to keep up a façade for the sake of the family or career. They don't think they have a good reason to be down, and they wonder what's wrong with them. What's wrong is that they are living from their should universe and not their internal universe.

The should universe also shows up when you think you need to do something a certain way. Even though you may feel tension and may put off following through for as long as possible, you force yourself to accomplish the task in the way you had planned because you are so fixated on doing it the way you "should." This happened to me when I was organizing a retreat that included restorative yoga. I thought I "should" practice the sequence I planned to teach. All day, I was thinking, "I should do this," but I never did. All day, I felt a discomfort inside of me that I couldn't shake. Finally, towards the end of the day, I realized that I was disconnected from my soul. I decided to leave the should universe and check in. I came to find out that I didn't want to do the sequence at all; I wanted to just do one pose, savasana, for an extended period of time. As soon as I realized this, I felt as though a weight had been lifted off of me. I didn't have to keep pushing to do what I thought I "should" do! I did savasana for forty-five minutes, and it felt great.

To see if you are occupying the should universe, contemplate these questions:

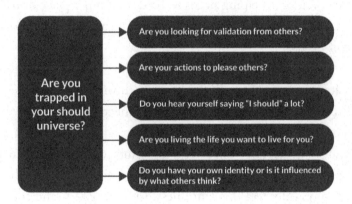

Are you trapped in your should universe?

- Are you looking for validation from others?
- Are your actions to please others?
- Do you hear yourself saying "I should" a lot?
- Are you living the life you want to live for you?
- Do you have your own identity or is it influenced by what others think?

THE OTHERS UNIVERSE

If you're living in the *others universe,* you are spending your time and mental energy focused on the lives of others rather than your own life. There are three categories of people who occupy the others universe:

- Overhelpers
- Binge TV/Netflix watchers
- Social media addicts and gossips

Overhelpers are consumed by other people's lives at the expense of their own. Most of their time and mind power is consumed with thinking about and helping others. These people often move from feeling the positive feelings that result from this dedication to feeling resentful and burnt out as a result of neglecting their own lives and needs. If you are an overhelper, you don't have to stop helping others; helping others can be one of the most satisfying activities in life. However, that helping needs to be done from a place of balance where you are also mindful about taking care of your own needs.

Binge TV watchers often feel like they are a part of a television program. They live vicariously through the characters, often to the point where they lose connection to themselves. People who fall into this category often tell me that they feel empty inside. They have been disconnected from their core for so long and are so far away from their center that they can physically feel this emptiness. Of course, TV and social media are common ways for us to take mental breaks. This is fine; just keep in mind that when you start feeling down or sensing an emptiness inside, the distraction you are using is taking you even further away from your soul. The uncomfortable feeling you're experiencing is your soul calling you to come back and connect to it.

People obsessed with social media and gossip spend their time talking about other people's lives. A certain amount of interest in other people is healthy. However, it becomes a problem when you make other people's lives more important than yours. In the process of consuming yourself with their lives, you may start feeling empty, lost, or like you're missing out on something. This emptiness comes from being disconnected from yourself for too long by putting too much attention on others. Because this universe does not usually trigger people like the previously described universes, it can be quite easy to get out of. All you need to do is recognize this "off" feeling. Then, by taking time to check in and connect with yourself, you will feel better.

To see if you are stuck in the others universe, think about these questions:

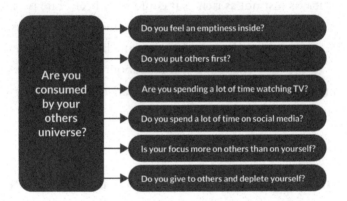

The world presents outside of ourselves. We are always interacting with it, and it unknowingly separates us from ourselves. We start to feel this separation when we get trapped outside of our internal universe.

Life is an active, alive process that we must live from moment to moment. Living any other way will not feel rich or fulfilling. If you are looking for true healing and transformation, you must let go of these four mind-created universes where language, categorization, absolute beliefs, and outward focus dominate and, instead, fully experience what is happening in the moment.

I equate this "real living" to sex. We have all had that amazing sexual experience where we were lost in the moment. There was no thinking; there was only the fullness of the experience—an amazing feeling. We have also had the kind of sex where we were thinking about what we were going to eat, going over our to-do list, and wondering if we were thin enough or if the other person liked us enough. It was sex, yes; but it was just not as rich as it could have been. Life is much the same. You can live life fully immersed in its juiciness, or you can live life half-there, having a mediocre experience.

In the next chapter, I will talk about how to connect to your internal universe so that you can fully experience the fullness of your life.

CONTEMPLATION: MIND-CREATED UNIVERSES

Reflect on the day you have had up until this moment.

Have you spent any time in any of these mind-created universes? Or all of them?

Which of the mind-created universes do you tend to slide into?

What are a few phrases you might hear yourself say or behaviors that you might see yourself engage in that can indicate to you that you've left your internal universe?

CHAPTER 7

HOW TO GET BACK
TO YOUR INTERNAL UNIVERSE

The first thing I want to make clear is that connecting to your internal universe does not take time. You don't need to work through all the issues you've accumulated over the course of your life. You don't need to learn how to trust yourself or create a self-help to-do list to stay on track. All of these steps are unnecessary—and they all originate from a mind-created universe.

Your internal universe is who you are. Connecting to your internal universe means you are allowing your soul—which is who you really are—to help you navigate life.

Navigating life from your soul will allow you to treat new situations very differently from the way you may have treated them in the past. Instead of letting your mind run wild and come up with an abundance of scenarios to make your way through an unknown or uncomfortable situation, simply identify what is actually happening in the moment and then connect to your internal universe for guidance. That's it. You will have confidence and clarity to move forward because you will be going with what's actually happening and what you're actually feeling rather than moving away from what is happening by analyzing the situation and picking it apart. When you are connected to your soul, you move through new situations with ease and enjoy your life no matter what external event is pending resolution.

Your soul knows how to do this thing called life. It is not the least bit worried about making mistakes or about not being sure how to proceed. It is not scared of the unknown because it lives in the moment—which is always known.

I was asked once, "If I am in my internal universe, connecting to my soul and dwelling entirely in the present moment, aren't I avoiding my real issues?" I believe that when you are busy with what seem to be your "real" issues, you are actually avoiding your present moment experience. What is happening now is the only real thing. Think about it. What's more real: where you are or what's in your mind?

You can't be in two places at once. You are either in your internal universe or not.

Remember that you are the main character of everything you see, feel, and experience. Therefore, connecting to yourself is your home base as you navigate this thing called life. Knowing how to get to your home base—your internal universe—how to stay there, and how to listen to its guidance will give you the ease and grace to move through the world in the best possible way.

I didn't always know this.

When I decided to finally figure out how to live from my internal universe, I was in a lot of emotional turmoil over the breakup and financial issues mentioned earlier. While I was shocked that my boyfriend had left the country and decided to stop talking to me, I was even more stunned by the fact that he shut down my website—one he had been hosting for my psychotherapy practice—without telling me. I couldn't stop thinking about what he had done, and it was all I could talk about with my friends.

I was stuck in a mind-created universe.

Knowing I was stuck in a mind-created universe didn't help me get out of it, however. I recognized that my suffering must have been the result of disconnection from my center. I also realized that connecting to my soul must be possible. It is who I really am. But I was not accustomed to living this way and didn't know how to get there.

Since the soul is who I really am, I realized, "The process of connecting to my soul has to be an organic and natural one." So, I decided to get clear about where I was in that present moment, even if I was in a mind-created universe. I knew that the soul is in the here and now, so the present moment must be the best place to start. To get clear on where I was, I identified the thoughts and feelings that were going on for me. I used "I feel" sentences like this: "I feel _____ because of _____, and therefore, _____.

The "I feel" sentences I came up with in the midst of my emotional turmoil were:

- "I feel stupid because this guy was able to hurt me, and therefore, I keep putting myself down," and

- "I feel angry at myself because I showed poor judgment with this guy, and therefore, I don't trust myself."

I wrote these down, and they led to more. I kept writing "I feel" sentences until something happened: I found the one that was really bothering me. It was the one above, the one about being angry at myself for trusting this guy and losing trust in myself. I instantly felt better! Instead of having thoughts and feelings swarming around in my head, I pinpointed what was really bothering me, and my mind was able to relax, at least for the moment.

I recognized that this process was the key to getting out of the universe I was stuck in. And it definitely offered relief.

* * *

If you are in a situation that causes you to get stuck in a mind-created universe, try creating "I feel" sentences around the situation. Write as many as come to mind, and then look them over and see which one of these sentences is the one that is "taking you out"—meaning it's the one your mind is trying to protect you from seeing and feeling. That's the one that is really bothering you. You will feel some relief when you find it.

* * *

Although I felt a bit better, the feeling didn't last. I still felt stuck. My mind-created universe just continued to try to find reasons why this breakup had happened and to figure out how I could make sure it never happened again. The loop of thought just kept going. I tried to stop it by telling myself to "get over it." I said things like, "There is no way I could have known this would happen," or "It was good that I took a chance on him." But all of these thoughts came from the mind-created universe—the one I had been freed from momentarily when I'd stated what was bothering me. There I was, roped back in.

This put me in a bind. On the one hand, I could see what I was doing; on the other hand, I had no control over it.

I spent some time not knowing what to do and getting swept up into thoughts and the associations that come along with them. I jumped from one universe to the other and just watched it all unfold.

And then, a curious thing happened. While I was watching my mind do all of this, I felt a bit of relief. This made me think that the watching could be a key to getting out. So, I started observing my thoughts and emotions, just getting to know them. When I got caught up in a thought, it would sweep me back in. But when I just watched it from afar, I could see it without getting caught up in it. I started doing that more often, and when a thought tried to grab me, I stubbornly put pressure between my eyes and stayed put, observing it from afar. This pressure between my eyes helped me stay in the present, watching my mind try to pull me back.

Our eyes are the keys to identifying and shifting the universe we live in. In a mind-created universe, our eyes are focused outward. We judge ourselves based on the outcome of an outside event. We also remain busy wondering why someone did something, how they feel, and what will happen next—all things that exist outside of ourselves. This creates anxiety because we end up trying to influence people and events that are outside our realm of control. In addition, focusing outward disperses our energy in many directions rather than maintaining our home base as the focal point of our energy and perspective.

When our eyes are focused externally, it is very easy to forget the person doing the seeing. We typically focus on the item being seen and not the person seeing. That person, "you," gets so caught up in what you see that you translate life through it. That translation can take over and keep you from remembering that you and your life are much bigger than the specific experience you are having. The event has passed, so now you are primarily experiencing thoughts about the event in the mind-created universe, which disconnects you from your center. Your eyes and mind are fully engaged in replaying and rehashing what occurred, but your body and soul are left out of the experience.

When I was thinking about my ex, my eyes were focused outward, on him. This made it very easy to forget about my soul. My feelings were all in reaction to him and what he did, and therefore, they were from a mind-created universe. So, I used the technique of putting pressure in between my eyes and imagined them turning inward to bring myself back toward my internal universe.

✳ ✳ ✳

Let's practice this.

Think of a time when you were trying to finish an email, and someone standing nearby kept interrupting you and keeping you from completing the task. You concentrated on that email and put your hand up to stop the other person from talking. Perhaps you even put pressure between your eyes to stay focused on your task.

This is very similar.

As you feel yourself having an emotion—for example, worrying—take a moment to turn your eyes inward. This process can be done with your eyes open or closed, so do what is easiest for you. Use your first two fingers and gently apply pressure on the spot right between your eyes. Now, stay put, right where you are in this very second, but remove your hand. Without your fingers, maintain this pressure between the eyes with the focus of your eyes inward. If you find yourself getting pulled into any of your thoughts and emotions, return to the pressure between your eyes and observe the movement of your mind and emotions from that vantage point. If it is very difficult to stay with the pressure between your eyes and you keep finding yourself in a mind-created universe, say the "I feel" sentence you are experiencing (this is what we did in the previous exercise) as you continue to place the pressure on the spot between your eyes. Tell your mind that it doesn't need to process this situation, that your soul has got this.

This inward focus is the start of your journey toward your internal universe.

* * *

While keeping pressure between my eyes and turning my eyes inward, I watched the movement of what was happening rather than busying myself with every thought and feeling I was having. This started the journey back to my internal universe. I saw the habitual patterns of my mind and my body's reactions to them. "This is my predicament," I told myself. "These are the habits I created. I am not going to worry about this. I will just allow my soul to see all this with no disturbance so that it can help me navigate through."

At some point, the dust settled, and my body and mind relaxed. I could feel myself again. I was able to breathe freely and feel my soul. I could hear my inner voice. Its guidance was telling me what my next best step towards feeling better was.

I started practicing this more and more. Soon, I could clearly see that my thoughts and emotions were not *me*. They were just there, and they came and went when I didn't engage with them. The ones that lingered, I came to discover, had some information for me. Usually, it was something I needed to address that I was trying to ignore, or something I was denying myself that I really wanted. The rest of the thoughts came out of nowhere and weren't triggering in any way. Sometimes, they were enjoyable to think—like when I pondered how something might go my way or daydreamed about something that would be fun to do. I would, at times, entertain myself with strange thoughts, funny thoughts, happy thoughts, scary thoughts. Other times, I found myself having conversations with people, telling them the same thing I'd already told them fifty times in my mind. But these thoughts didn't disturb me. This made me wonder if there was really a problem with these thoughts. After all, they didn't create webs of associations, judgments, and beliefs; they were just me talking to myself.

I realized that I could think these thoughts consciously and be in my internal universe thinking, or I could be thinking them unconsciously and be disconnected from my internal universe and my present moment experience. So, although these thoughts weren't triggering in any way, they could disconnect me from my soul if I wasn't aware of being stuck in thought rather than in the present moment. The key was being aware and knowing where I was when I was thinking the thoughts.

I started to categorize my thoughts. I noticed that I had thoughts that entangled me and made me suffer as a result of their associations and judgments. They kept me engaged in analysis and created their own universe. Then, I had thoughts that kept me occupied with daydreaming, reminiscing, and replaying. These thoughts didn't make me suffer, but they did disconnect me from the present moment. I had thoughts that just popped up; these emerged, were noticed, and then disappeared. I saw that I had a commentator voice that talked to me as though it was the emcee of a ceremony. I had contemplative thoughts that wondered and questioned. Finally, I had thoughts that arose from within—intuitive thoughts.

All of these thoughts serve a purpose: They let you know where you are and how you are doing.

If you are in your mind-created universes, you are disconnected from your center and most likely not feeling good. If you are preoccupied with thought, you are not present. You might not be feeling bad, but you're not fully living. Your mind, body, and soul are not aligned. If thoughts are popping up and drifting in and out, you are present and understanding that the constant flow of thoughts has become a habit because that's how you have been taught to live life. You have gotten used to living life this way and, therefore, it has become part of your daily routine. If you are the commentator, you are attached to talking about what is happening rather than experiencing it. In this case, you are slightly disconnected from your center. If you are having contemplative thoughts, you can be connected to your center if you ask a question and then listen for the answer. If you start trying to figure it out by going into tangents and associations, then you're disconnected from your soul. If you are having intuitive thoughts pop up, that means you are connected to your soul and getting guidance.

As I practiced categorizing thoughts and observing where I was when I was having them, I got good at recognizing when I was externally focused and then choosing to come back to the soul.

One morning, after I'd been working on this for a while, I was drinking my cup of coffee and writing, as I often do. A new guy who had just entered my life came into my mind. I found him confusing because he had strong energy and often played games. Just thinking about him pulled me into turmoil. I knew that if I stayed in the turmoil and fed it, I would get trapped in a universe outside of my internal universe. Which universe I got trapped in would depend on the thoughts I fed. If I focused on what *he* was doing, I would get trapped in my external universe. If I wondered what was wrong with *me* that encouraged him to play games or thought about how I wasn't good enough or could never keep a guy, then I would be stuck in my alternate universe. If I said, "He *should* call," or, "I *should* be sweeter to him," then I would be stuck in my should universe. Finally, if I checked social media or watched television to forget about him and my life, I would get stuck in the others universe. Rather than following any of these thought patterns, what I could do— and what I decided to do—was just allow the thought and any feeling associated with it to show up and then leave. That allowed me to stay connected to my internal universe and continue writing and enjoying my coffee.

This sounds so simple. And, actually, it is—but it can be difficult to do because of our conditioning. We are taught to listen to our thoughts and feelings, process them, analyze them, and believe them. These actions interfere with the self-navigation system that exists inside of us.

No matter what the situation is or how intense the emotion is, your soul knows how to navigate through it. When thoughts and feelings are very intense and don't just come and go, the key is to ride the roller coaster of that emotion. I'll go into more detail about that in a later chapter.

CHAPTER 8

THOUGHT LOOPS

Before I learned the importance of reconnecting to my soul, when I felt down or anxious, I would try to make myself feel better by exercising, doing yoga, calling a friend, or watching television. Basically, I did anything I could to cope with the situation—which often assumed the form of taking my mind off what I was worried about and/or changing the energy around it. This worked, but only temporarily. A little while later or the next day, I would find myself feeling the same way. It seems logical now why these distractions didn't work: I was acting from a universe outside my internal universe as a reaction to the thoughts and feelings of that disconnected universe. Therefore, when I was done with my coping behavior, I was back where I started—in a mind-created universe. Nothing had been accomplished other than experiencing a bit of relief.

I equate these distracting behaviors to being in a room and moving furniture around to get a different perspective or insight. All you're doing is taking everything in the room and shifting its location. Nothing really changes. On the other hand, when you leave the mind-created universe you're in, you are essentially opening the door of that room and allowing yourself to work with the whole of existence. Much more information is available to you as you consider solutions. Your internal universe is the key to tapping into those solutions.

Like many people, I enjoy processing and analyzing things. That's okay—until processing and analyzing becomes a never-ending loop. The way out of the loop is not trying to resolve the issue. This is because it's not the issue that is really the problem; it's the universe you created around the issue. The issue itself, in its raw form without distortion of thought, is solvable. Therefore, the way out is to end the loop and reestablish connection to the internal universe, your home of solutions and guidance. Once I do this, I feel calmer, clearer, and better overall.

Sometimes, the loop is strong, and you won't be able to stop it. When this happens, identify the thoughts and emotions that keep repeating—like you did as part of the exercise in the previous chapter. This is an important step because your mind creates universes in order to avoid feeling the discomfort of what is truly bothering you. Once you identify the real issue, you will feel more relaxed. Think about one of those conversations with a friend where you are talking and talking about your boyfriend/husband, children, or job that is bothering you. You talk in circles because you are so upset—and then, suddenly, you hit on the thing that is actually bothering you, and you no longer need to talk about it. You relax right away because you have gotten to your truth— the truth that was covered up by your mind. This is exactly what will happen when you identify the thoughts and feelings that are truly bothering you in the moment.

Loops can be especially strong in people who have a history of trauma. Typically, during a traumatic event, you have no control and no ability to defend yourself, get away, or express your feelings. Sometimes, you don't even recognize what's happening until later, when your body reacts to it. Sometimes, you repress the memory and are shocked when it is recalled later. In any case, the trauma is distressing, so your mind tries to protect you from this discomfort by disconnecting you from your body, where you feel the trauma. You are, at this point, mainly living in your head.

People often tell me that they self-sabotage because of their trauma. For example, they tell me that they pick fights with their partner to avoid getting hurt again. Although the self-sabotage may be due to the trauma, it is not the reason the self-sabotage—and the misery it causes—is occurring in the present. If you're self-sabotaging in the present, it's a result of the universe you created after the trauma occurred. This universe is made up! You experienced a trauma and created a universe because of that trauma. Being stuck in that universe is what perpetuates the cycle, not the trauma itself.

Here's an example from my life. When I was young, my mom desperately wanted me to be thin. She was emotionally and sometimes even physically abusive towards me, all in the guise of caring for me. When I was just eight years old, she put me on a diet. Her actions resulted in my becoming a compulsive overeater and my sister, who witnessed the trauma I went through, becoming anorexic. In my twenties, I did therapy, emotional release work, primal work, hypnosis—everything I could come up with. I screamed, expressed, and confronted my mom. I knew exactly why I overate, but still, I couldn't break the cycle. While I did quit overeating in anger or to hurt myself, I still overate.

My overeating only stopped completely when I realized that I was barking up the wrong tree. I was trying to resolve something from the past by trying to heal the inner child who had been hurt by this trauma. The trauma had created a whole universe of associations and judgments, and I was moving from that mind-created universe. This inner work was done from a disconnected mind-created universe, and spending time in that universe—even under the guise of healing—kept me trapped there. The only way to truly resolve my overeating issues once and for all was to leave the universe I created around them.

It is important to note that, although you are only in one universe at a time, an event can create multiple universes. To avoid getting caught up in figuring out what universe you are in, I like to keep it simple: Either you are in your internal universe, or you're not. You can only find your way out when you are in your internal universe.

I have no food issues these days. I can have junk food in my house and not eat it all up. For the most part, I crave healthy food, and I eat with a great appetite and enjoy my meals.

If you find that you are feeling burnt out, like you want to put your life on pause, or that you need a break, this feeling is telling you that you are pushing too hard and moving in the wrong direction—away from your internal universe. Feeling overwhelmed and thinking your life has become unmanageable are signs that it's time to come back to your soul and connect. In addition, if the thoughts you're thinking and speaking about are contradictory to what you want, you are stuck in a universe that isn't your internal universe.

The way forward is always the same: Identify that you are in a universe outside of your internal universe, then take the journey back to your soul.

Unfortunately, we don't always realize that we are stuck in a mind-created universe because it feels so natural to be there. The situation is all we can see, and it envelops our whole mind, encouraging us to think that there is something that needs to change in order for us to feel better. We believe we need to do something or that another person needs to do something so that things can change. Sometimes this is true; if that's the case, do what you need to do and resolve the situation. But if something isn't right, and you have done what you can but still keep replaying thoughts in your mind or feel consumed by negative feelings, you're stuck in a mind-created universe.

"But it takes time to process and change," some people say. "I have been triggered by a trauma. It's my old patterns. I need time to heal." They think they have so much to heal from that they're willing to struggle for days, weeks, or even months. I used to think this way. Now I know that our ability to feel better in this very second is in us and around us at all times.

At first, I didn't grasp the significance of this realization. I would move from being very upset to finding peace by simply taking a breath or petting my cat. "How is this possible?" I wondered. "A moment ago, I was totally overwhelmed and upset. Now, in this moment, I feel so relaxed. Is it really this easy?" Initially, I thought the action of petting my cat or breathing was what created the relief. But when I did those actions deliberately to generate relief, they didn't work. This had me perplexed.

It wasn't the action that was healing me. The action worked because I was led to do what would help me in that moment. I tuned into my soul, and my soul provided guidance. That's why it worked.

With that realization, I saw that the possibility of feeling good was available even when the situation wasn't resolved. I no longer bought into those old ideas—that the process takes time, that I needed to change something, that someone else needed to change something, that the outside situation needed to change. I knew in my gut that none of that had to occur for me to feel good. I grasped that there is a part of me, my soul, that isn't caught up in any one situation; it just moves with life.

Catch a glimpse of it, and you will never want to move from any place else.

CHAPTER 9

FREEDOM FROM THE MIND-CREATED UNIVERSES

The difference between living from your soul and living from your mind lies in your perspective. Your soul understands that all experiences are possible in life. It also knows that when an event occurs, that's all it is—a momentary occurrence. It does not create a thought that tries to make it better by looking at the bright side or explaining how or why the experience needs to be fixed, nor does it claim that this is *always* how it will be. It doesn't create webs of what-ifs or future scenarios. The soul just experiences the experience and moves on.

The mind, on the other hand, creates universes by taking an event or an emotion and denying it with justifications, by looking for the positive spin to avoid the authentic emotion, or by making an absolute out of it. "I will *always* feel disappointed," it says. "It is bad to feel uncomfortable. I must get rid of this discomfort because it will interfere with the rest of my day. This isn't fair. Why does this always happen to me? I'll never get it…," and so on. From those absolutes, we create stories and beliefs. These trap us into living in a mind-created universe where we analyze, interpret, fix, and try to change the thoughts and emotions that we formed based on the event that happened. We believe what we are thinking because we created this universe from a real moment that did occur and from a thought that may well be true for that experience. However, we can have many different moments in life. What is true for one moment may not be true for another moment. The soul knows that—which is why it has no problem experiencing every moment in time just as it is.

If you find yourself caught in a thought loop, you are in a mind-created universe. Instead of dealing with the facts of the situation, you are dealing with a fake universe made up around the facts.

This is crucial to understand. Most people think what happens to them causes them misery. In reality, anything that happens in life occurs in one moment in time. In the next moment, it does not exist in the same way. A moment can be unpleasant, but it always passes. Misery and suffering are what we feel when we don't allow the unpleasant experience to be felt and fully experienced. "Fully experiencing" a moment could mean crying, screaming, laughing, or being silent—as long as it's expressing what is occurring in that moment in an authentic way. Your soul doesn't judge how you express or experience life; it just observes and self-navigates toward peace and joy. When you don't allow the moment to unfold in its totality and instead build a mind-created universe around it, you will carry misery and suffering with you. You will also miss each moment of your life because of your preoccupation with the previous one. The present moment always presents a new possibility; that's why it is so important to move with each moment. That is what truly living life means!

* * *

Let's pause so you can really experience the moment you're in.

Turn your eyes inward—either by putting pressure on your third eye, like you did previously when you touched the point between your eyebrows, or by placing pressure behind your eyes, imagining that you are seeing from the back of your eyes. This creates a bit of space between you and what you are seeing.

While you're doing this, see if you can also sense all the other things around you that are occurring in this moment. These include your thoughts, sensations, sounds, and actions. Think of this like having the TV on in the background at your house. As you're doing chores, every so often, you notice something that happened on the TV. You watch it and then come back to what you were doing.

The practice of being present and noticing everything around you might look like this: *You are making breakfast. Your mind is pulling you into a negative thought. You feel a lurch in the pit of your stomach. You hear the cars outside. You become aware again that you are making breakfast. The thought comes back. You are eating breakfast. You feel an emptiness inside. You get in your car.* You get the idea.

Practice this now. Feeling your eyes turned inward, observe casually everything that is occurring in this moment. Make this process of observing complete. You are not just witnessing your thoughts and feelings and then turning inward; your eyes are turned inward, and you are aware of all aspects of your life. That includes everything that is happening in this moment—which is a lot.

We so often get sucked into our universe and into trying to change it that we forget about all the life that is happening now, moment to moment, all around us, all the time.

* * *

Imagine that you are at a party, and people are in the kitchen insulting the host and criticizing the food. Trying to stop them from doing this would be exhausting. You decide to leave the kitchen and go to the living room. You may still be able to hear them there, but you won't be engaging with them. If what you hear affects you, feel it. At the same time, you can keep enjoying the party despite the presence of those feelings in the background. You can deal with your mind-created universes in a similar way. Notice your thoughts, but don't engage with them. Include them in the present moment as one of the many things that are occurring.

The solution to all of your internal turmoil is not to fight with the mind-created universe or try to change it. Just leave it.

There was a time in my life when I always felt like I was screwing up. I was convinced I had to figure out how to be a better person. I couldn't relax, get clear, or be sure. I was always working on something within myself, trying to stay positive, love others, and be inclusive. I wasn't okay with how I felt or what I thought. I believed that I needed to be different. And as a result, I was always in a state of internal conflict. I didn't understand that all of my emotions and thoughts were and are always valid. It's okay to think and feel everything!

In time, I came to realize that what I thought and felt was a gauge of what was happening inside of me. These thoughts and feelings were indicators that could provide very important information, not things that needed to be fought, changed, or pushed aside. They told me that something internal was missing and that this missing piece needed to be addressed. For example, one day, when I was driving, I found myself feeling anxious and wanting to kill everyone on the road. This was an indicator that it was time for me to "clean up" inside and figure out what was really bothering me. The way I did this was by asking myself, "Debbie, what is it that you need now?"

This question, "What is it that you need now?" shifts the focus to your internal universe and helps you connect to your soul to find out what it is that you need.

After looking inward, I discovered that I was hungry. I had gotten so busy that I hadn't eaten in six hours, and my hunger was the real source of my anxiety, not the other people on the road. This was not a thinking process with questions and analysis; it was more of an "allowing" process. I got my mind out of the way so that my soul could see what was going on and let me know what was needed.

When you look inside, you'll often find that something is missing—and that something is often unrelated to the thought or emotion that showed up. You can only realize this when you allow the full expression of your emotions and the unedited thinking of your thoughts without making them wrong or getting carried away with them by creating meanings, stories, or absolutes. Feeling and thinking whatever shows up without being attached to it or engaging in it will allow you to discover your truth. Your truth gives you access to the information that helps you uncover what you need. That information is for your soul to see, not for your mind to explain and interpret.

One of the obstacles we face when trying to feel what we're feeling is fear. Emotions scare a lot of people, and we're often told at a young age to keep them under wraps. "Don't laugh so loud," my father used to say. My mom told me I was too tough, and my teachers told me I was too sensitive. Many of my clients were told that sadness and crying are signs of weakness. It took many years and lots of emotional release work, breath work, and primal work for me to be able to express my emotions unapologetically. And, even with all of that practice, I still had trouble expressing my emotions in the moment for many years. What I had to learn was to just allow them. I needed to learn to witness my emotions without trying to change them. When the dust settles, I ask myself, "Is there any information here for me to learn from? Do I want something to be different?" If so, I look at what that is and imagine that difference. Then I ask myself, "What is needed for this situation to be different?" Whatever answer

I get, I play with in my life. And it really is play—not resistance, not fighting, not fixing what's wrong.

When you allow thoughts and feelings to happen without getting carried away by them, you can use them as information and begin to flow with life.

CHAPTER 10

USING THE BODY'S WISDOM TO GET BACK TO THE SOUL

The mind is tricky. It can fool us into thinking we are doing well when we are actually really off-course. Your best gauge is always how you feel inside. If your mind is quiet and you are flowing through life with ease, you are connected to your soul.

After I left Judaism and went traveling, I came back to New York because my grandmother was dying. I got to spend time with her before she passed. Then, shortly afterward, I left New York to live in Florida. When I was with my family, I played the religious game so as not to hurt them. Once I moved to Florida, I was able to live the life I wanted, freely. I was free from religion and away from my family, but I was still trapped in my mind. My body was still reacting to triggers and thoughts.

I was trying to explore the world, but my old conditioning kept coming back. I heard it in the words I said to myself: "Don't do that," "You can't accomplish that," "Stop wasting time," "Try harder," "Do more," and so on. I thought I was free, but although I didn't realize it, I was still trapped.

The thoughts in your mind are subtle and can easily be missed, but the body always lets you know what's going on. You freeze, your body tenses up, you feel resistance inside, you feel uncomfortable. It feels unsafe for you to express and explore your emotions, so you hold them in. This creates tension in your body, which, in turn, causes you to create a way of thinking and acting that enables you to avoid those emotions. This avoidance disconnects you from your center, your soul, your internal universe and puts you in a mind-created universe. Your body literally tells you when this is happening—if you listen to it.

※　※　※

Take a moment now to see how you are feeling in your body.

Freeze right where you are. Don't change anything, and just notice.

Is there tension anywhere in your body? How are you breathing—slowly, deeply, rapidly? Can you feel your breath? Can you feel the couch you're sitting on? Do you feel any sensations? Is your energy flowing or stuck/frenetic?

Remember, there's no need to judge any of these observations or to make any changes to them. You're just noticing, learning to observe.

※　※　※

Through my experimentation, I realized that when I felt relaxed inside, in my core, I was on track. I also began to understand that even when I was feeling relaxed and in my internal universe, superficial emotions and sensations could be present. "Superficial" emotions are the ones that are present and move around but don't get stuck. We are energy beings that are in constant motion, and we are always interacting with the environment. As a result, we sense many things all the time. This is not a problem! You can treat these emotions the way you treat everything else in the environment: by letting your internal self-navigating system—the one that's built into your body—do what it needs to do with it. Your system is programmed to work with the energy and sensations around you. Much like your system can self-heal when you get a cut, your system can self-navigate, so you don't have to do anything consciously.

I learned that allowing the energy and sensations to exist inside without interference was key to having a healthy self-navigation system—one that could communicate with my soul and allow it to tell me what is needed in my life. In my exploration of my internal world, I learned that energy in the body typically shows up as sensations, tensions, and vibrations. These can clearly indicate to us where our focus is, so a good way to see where you are living is to determine where you feel the most energy or pressure in your body.

For the sake of simplicity, think of yourself as mind, heart, and center—or, as is more commonly said—mind, body, and soul. At any point in time, your energy is concentrated in one of these three areas:

- on the top of your body/in your head,

- in the middle of your body/in your heart/in your solar plexus, or

- in your lower body/in your pelvis/in your lower belly.

The higher the energy is, the more dispersed it is. The lower the energy is, the more rooted it is. When my energy is in my lower belly or pelvis, I am moving from a grounded and centered place—my internal universe. When my energy is in my heart or solar plexus, I am moving from my emotions, a reaction generated from the mind-created universe. When my energy is in my head, I am moving from my mind-created universe.

Lowering your energy needs to be a gradual process. It typically involves the eyes, as the eyes help direct energy. When I notice that I'm stuck in my head, I keep my eyes looking inward. This creates a feeling of pressure in my third eye. There is no force and no push; there is only the intention of looking inward. When I keep it long enough, I can feel a wave of warmth fill my body. I feel a tingling. In that moment, I know I am connected to the whole of who I am. A deep breath occurs inside—but I don't take that breath; it happens spontaneously. That breath is another indicator that I am connected to my center, my soul.

✻ ✻ ✻

Don't take my word for it. Play with this to see for yourself!

Check to see where your energy is right now. Is it in your head, heart, or center?

Check again periodically throughout the day. When you get tense, notice where your energy is. When you are relaxed, notice where it is. Get to know your energy.

* * *

The process is always the same. If your energy is in your head or your solar plexus/heart area, the only thing to do is turn your eyes inward and observe it. Don't try to change it; instead, watch it like a ping-pong ball as it moves around. Follow it with your eyes. You may notice some rapid blinking happening spontaneously. If so, allow it. Keep watching and allowing the rapid blinking until it naturally stops. You will then feel relief. At that point, take a deep breath into your lower belly/pelvis area and let the energy settle there.

This is your body telling you that you have returned to your internal universe. You are, once again, connected to your soul. Enjoy that feeling.

CHAPTER 11

THE MIND/BODY/SOUL BALANCE

We've already talked a bit about the mind, the body, and the soul. Living in only one of them will leave you feeling unfulfilled. It's important to maintain a balance among the three. Let's look a little more closely at how they each work and, more importantly, how they work together.

THE MIND

The mind is something we have been given. It comes with our body, and it lasts for a short time here on Earth. It is not who we are—although we often make it who we are.

Like any other organ in the body, the mind operates automatically. Our mind sends messages to our body continuously without guidance. Yes, we can think consciously, much like we can take a breath consciously—but even if we don't think, the brain is working. It is picking up information from our environment and communicating it to the rest of our body. Our mind then comes in and interprets and analyzes that information—more out of habit than out of necessity.

Personally, I think that the mind is supposed to communicate silently with our body and our soul. Perhaps language has created a misuse of the mind since we now talk to ourselves incessantly, repetitively, and unnecessarily. We would never tolerate this amount of chatter from anyone else, but for some reason, we allow our mind to talk nonstop—and we listen and believe what it says most of the time. This mind chatter creates a huge barrier for communication to and from the soul. It also interferes with clear observation of and perspective on what is happening around us since our mind, when engaged, tends to go into analyzing, projecting, and remembering, rather than sticking to just seeing and responding.

Krishnamurti, a twentieth-century Indian philosopher who wrote extensively about the mind, speaks about it as being a tool for science. He describes how the mind is good for building things. When it comes to psychological matters, however, the mind is not helpful because it is always trying to figure out the past. Your life is happening now, not in the past. Krishnamurti also talks about the difference between observing and thinking. Thinking, he says, is like having a veil of memories, judgments, and beliefs in front of your eyes, keeping you from seeing the reality in front of you. Observing is seeing directly, without the veil. By observing without thinking, Krishnamurti says we can be completely present in our experiences and able to see reality for what it truly is.

The mind has greater capabilities than we know when directed by our soul. It has the power to create and the power to heal. It can tap into universal wisdom and communicate on a deeper level. In doing so, it can assist us in going in the direction we want to go.

THE BODY

The body is our vehicle in this life. It's our way to conduct activity in this world. It's also our way to connect to our internal GPS system. We must go through the body to connect to our soul. We must be willing to fully experience life—including all the emotions, sensations, and experiences that come along with it. The ability to be in our body and live each moment fully allows us to ground into our lower energy center, settle into our core, and connect to our soul.

There's a great scene in the movie *Good Will Hunting* where Will is told that he can read books and "think he knows things," but he can really only know anything from real experience. Real experience is felt in the body.

Interestingly, in our culture, many people care very deeply about their appearances, but they don't seem to care as much about connecting to their bodies. Instead, they live in their minds—which, as we've discussed, is not where experience occurs. Often, when we're having experiences, we speak about them. If you are speaking, you are not feeling or experiencing. Speaking is an act of the mind, not of the body.

THE SOUL

Your soul is your connection to the essence of who you are and the world around you. It embodies the subtle aspects of who you are, much like the air in the room and the space between objects that we don't pay attention to. The qualities of life that aren't tangible or measurable, such as trust and love, are elements of the soul. The soul connects you to the universe because you *are* the universe. Your soul came here to have a human experience. It innately knows how to move through life with ease. Your soul is not afraid of any experience because it knows that an experience is just a moment in time. Life is constantly moving; it doesn't stay stuck in the past or even in the current moment. By the time you notice the current moment, it has already passed. Your soul is your authentic expression in the moment. It is not necessarily positive, but it is always genuine, grounded, and connected to the whole of who you are and the whole of life.

Embracing your mind, body, and soul is the key to embracing life. You must live a life that balances all three.

Here is an example of how I create balance between my soul, mind, and body. If I have a to-do list of items that needs to be completed, I check in with my soul to see which item on the list I'd like to start with. I keep checking in as the day goes on to see what I would like to do next. I also ask myself how I'd like to approach each task. I ask as though I have no idea what the answer might be. I then have my mind and body follow. So, although my mind and body are acting in life, my soul is guiding the way when I take the time to listen to it.

This approach has made life an adventure, an exploration. Each day is brand new instead of habitual and repetitive. This also helps me stay true to myself and flow with life.

I put my soul first; then, I let my mind help me set up the details and let my body follow through.

Another way I have learned to create soul, mind, and body balance and live a life of ease, joy, and fulfillment is by starting every action from my soul. How do I make sure to always do that? By simply observing experiences. For example, one day, I got upset because I forgot to record an important Zoom session. I felt a pit in my stomach, like I had screwed up. I let myself be upset, without judgment. I fully felt the emotion in my body while I remained alert and aware from my soul. Not more than a few minutes went by, and it just disappeared as though it never happened.

Rather than letting your mind and body take over with thoughts and emotions, you need to experience every event in life the way you experience stubbing your toe: Say, "Ouch," feel the annoyance of it and the pain in the toe, and keep doing what you were doing. You can feel the throb in your toe, notice it, and keep living your day.

The throbbing of a toe is just a part of our life; it is not our whole life. When you include it in your experience rather than letting it take over your reality or pushing it away, it will resolve naturally. You have been created with a soul that knows how to live life. It will take care of everything.

CHAPTER 12

HOW TO RIDE THE ROLLER COASTER OF EMOTIONS

It sounds easy enough: Just experience life and let it flow through you, past you, and around you. Watch what happens, and stay connected to the soul while doing so.

So, why don't we always do this? What goes wrong?

The problem arises when we get stuck in either the body or the mind by reacting to strong thoughts and emotions due to our attachments in life. Our belief in their significance causes us to give them meaning. When we do this, we disconnect from our soul. The key is staying connected to your soul as you are experiencing those thoughts and emotions in order to discover if something needs to be done or if the thoughts and emotions emerging are just waves passing through that don't warrant any attention or action.

You'll notice that I used the word *emotions,* not the word *feelings.* There is a huge difference between the two.

Emotions are energy in motion, and that's what they feel like: they are intense, they move through you, and then they're gone. You can't hold on to an emotion for too long because it will change on its own. Try to hold on to an emotion for even five minutes. I guarantee you won't be able to!

Feelings, on the other hand, can stay with you forever. Feelings are perpetuated by thoughts. If you think the same thought, you get the same feeling. When you watch the same movie over and over again, you will cry and laugh at the same scenes. In much the same way, you will have the same reaction each time you think the same thought.

Thoughts create feelings and block emotions. Feelings are actually thoughts misrepresented as emotions. For example, when you say, "I feel lonely," you are in the *thought* of loneliness and the story of it. You are not in the actual emotion—if you were, you'd be in your body. We do this often because it is easier to think about an emotion than to feel it, especially when the emotion is intense. The mind tries to "help" us by disconnecting us from the body and creating a mind-created universe.

CONTEMPLATION: FEELINGS AND EMOTIONS

Check in and see what you are feeling now.

How does it feel in your body?

Can you let yourself experience it in your body?

Or are you thinking about it with your mind?

I like to think about emotions like a Disneyland theme park renamed "Lifeland." We are all riding the different attractions of life, each of which creates its own emotion. Whatever ride we're on, we need to stay on. We need to hold on and ride the ride completely—which means we can't separate the ride from the emotion. The emotion needs to be included in the experience. If you're about to go to the doctor for your mammogram and feel scared, you are on the scared mammogram ride. Ride it exactly how you would ride a roller coaster. If you do that and avoid getting stuck in a mind-created universe, the ride will be intense, but it will end quickly. If you get stuck in a mind-created universe, on the other hand, then you will be in a loop of thought that will keep creating the same fear-based feeling for days, weeks, or months—even though it's not even a real emotion. The only thing that's real is this present moment. An emotion that shows up in this moment is real and should be ridden. That's all.

Let's look at an example of navigating this process of staying connected to the soul while riding the ride that is this life.

It was a Friday morning, and I woke up feeling off. I felt lonely. It seemed like I couldn't do anything right, which made me feel overwhelmed. I wanted to run and avoid these feelings. I had a fairly light client day planned, so I made a schedule for myself that included working out, dance practice, and writing. I started by working out and eating a healthy breakfast, but I still couldn't shake the discomfort. I spent a couple of hours in my ruminating mind-created universe. I wanted to distract myself but knew that my desire for distraction was just a sign of my disconnection.

Finally, I checked in with my energy. I noticed it was in my heart, swirling around. So, I breathed into it and just let it be. It revealed to me that I was upset. Yes, I felt lonely, but that wasn't what was really bothering me. My cat had been recently diagnosed with diabetes and, yes, I felt like I would never get my cat's insulin right. But that wasn't it either. I realized that the source of my upset was a conversation I'd had with a friend the day before. She said she wanted to travel and had no one to travel with, but she didn't even consider me as an option. This was not the first time she did something fun and didn't call me, and I started to think that, in her opinion, I was only good for advice and venting. I was hurt. This was the truth of my discomfort. Anything else was barking up the wrong tree. I was only able to access this information by checking in with my soul and not letting my mind or emotions take me into a mind-created universe. I took the "hurt ride" to its completion, allowing myself to feel it fully. Feeling it fully helped me access what I wanted in the long term, which was to go on vacations that I enjoy in my way. Then, I checked in to see what I needed in the moment, which turned out to be a bath. After the bath, what I needed was to discard my to-do list and write, and I did that too. And what do you know, I got back to a calm space! I had entered back into the flow of life. Nothing was resolved because there was nothing *to* resolve. This process isn't about resolution; it's about letting the soul lead the way and following its guidance. It's an inner game, not an outer game. When you master your inner game, the outer game follows.

CHAPTER 13

NAVIGATING INTERNAL CONFLICT

Thoughts and feelings can create tension within us. The way many of us were taught to deal with this tension is through reasoning. We were encouraged to analyze the thoughts and feelings we don't like and disprove the ones that are keeping us stuck. Sometimes this process can be useful, but once you feel anxiety, pressure, and uneasiness, you have disconnected from your internal universe and entered a mind-created universe.

If you start to pay attention to your thoughts, you will notice that, a lot of the time, you are creating conflict within yourself by either fighting who you are in this moment or fighting what is happening in your life. Any time you tell yourself to change, that you are not okay, or that you have to be different, you are creating internal conflict. You are who you are, and a part of you is telling yourself that you are not okay the way you are. Typically, this takes the form of thoughts like, "I am too fat," "I have to lose weight," "I can't look in the mirror," and "I can't stand myself." Think about this: Who are you talking to? Can you see how you are creating a conflict inside of you? Most people think that change occurs through this kind of self-talk. However, change can occur from love and direction rather than from hate and criticism.

Most of us sense this and have learned to be nicer to ourselves. We say things like, "It's okay," or "You have beautiful eyes." Or we use affirmations, like, "I am beautiful," or "I am getting thinner every day." But this creates conflict as well because now you are having a debate inside. Fighting with thoughts in your head creates anguish and discomfort. There is only one you, so when you debate yourself, you are essentially splitting yourself into opposing sides that fight with each other.

Debating with yourself—even if it is done in an effort to improve yourself—is an act of the mind-created universe. I like to compare it to arguing with a family member of mine who thinks she is always right. Do you have one of those? If you do, you know that it's exhausting and frustrating—and there's no way you can win. One of you will inevitably lose the debate.

In my psychotherapy practice, I used to help clients heal past wounds by going back to the initial event that created the wound and having them talk to their inner child. This is a beneficial and valid technique, but I came to realize that this process also creates inner conflict. Saying things to yourself that feel good is essentially talking to yourself as though you are more than just one person. This creates a division inside, which causes inner conflict. It also disconnects you from your soul and the present moment experience.

For example, if you are feeling scared, going into a past event where you felt scared and telling your inner child, "It's safe," takes you into a mind-created universe: the past. Instead, observe and experience the fear in the present and allow it to reveal whatever it needs to reveal. Your soul came here to experience all of life, and this includes fear. Your soul is not scared of this experience or any other. Once it is felt, the fear will pass. Also, by staying present, you will be able to check in to see what's needed in the moment and listen to the soul's guidance to know what to do next. This is the only way to get out of inner conflict, truly resolve past wounds, and stop the repetitive thinking that interferes with your peace and joy.

I have this saying: "If I say I don't care, that means I really do care, but I don't want to care." The reality is that if I really didn't care about something, it wouldn't even come to my mind to say that I don't care.

It's much the same with inner debate. If I feel the need to say, "I matter," it means I don't think I matter, but I *want* to matter. If I really believed that I mattered, I wouldn't have to say it. I use these statements as gauges to tell me where I am. If I'm trying to make myself feel or think a certain way, then I'm creating internal conflict. If I think I should be different than how I am in this present moment—even if that difference is an attempt at self-improvement—I am fighting with myself. This internal conflict is of the mind-created universe.

It has me going around in circles because, in this state, I'm disconnected from my soul.

You will know you are experiencing inner conflict when there is a feeling of resistance inside. People often think you need to push through this feeling, but that's not true! Life is to be enjoyed. When you love your life and what you are doing, you never need to push through anything. The discomfort or resistance you're feeling is an indication that you are moving in the wrong direction—away from your internal universe. You need to recognize that you are stuck in a mind-created universe and get out of it.

I have clients who tell me that they keep trying to maintain a "gratitude journal" but just can't follow through with it. "Gratitude is wonderful," I tell them, "but if you're looking for gratitude, it's not naturally coming from inside of you." They are continuously trying to find gratitude to feel better, and this is a process that comes from the mind-created universe. I suggest that they use gratitude as a gauge instead. If you aren't feeling grateful, you are stuck in a thought pattern that's making you feel that way. Check in to see what is needed so that gratitude flows through you naturally and spontaneously.

Krishnamurti speaks about conflict being a huge part of suffering, and I see this in my practice all the time. He says that conflict within yourself is one of the roots of suffering; the other is conflict with what is.

It is human to want people to act in the ways we want them to and situations to turn out how we want. In reality, though, this just creates conflict within us since we are reacting to something that happened and wishing it was different. But it is in the past and cannot be changed. We typically react to interactions and events that occur in our lives in this way and, in doing so, interfere with our self-navigation process.

We make the mistake of thinking that our reactions are the result of the interaction or event. They are not. The interaction or event triggers an emotional response, and we have feelings associated with that emotional response. Instead of feeling the primary emotion fully and working through whatever particular sadness or discomfort we're experiencing (that we have probably been carrying around for a long time), we defend it, process it, analyze it, and sometimes even feel guilty about it or resent it. What we don't understand is that we are not connected to the event. The event is a stand-alone occurrence; our reaction is our own experience. They are acts in the same play, but they are not connected in the causal way we typically assume. The event holds no big meaning that we need to look into and presents no story that we need to spin. All we need to do is use the event as a gauge to let us know how we feel. Our emotions provide information to our soul that helps us navigate our journey. In other words, the event is what is. To see it clearly and know how to respond, you must be able to separate the event from your reaction, allow the dust to settle, and then act or not act from there. By the time you notice what's happening, it's already in the past. Life is still going, even if you're busy fighting whatever already happened. This fighting creates inner conflict because, intuitively, you know there is nothing that can be done about a past event. Yet, your mind will not stop trying to figure out a resolution—something it cannot do since the event has already happened. Tension builds, your mind fixates on the event, and you become unhappy.

This may seem discouraging, but actually, it is extremely freeing. With the vast amount of people and opportunities available to experience in this world, the only way for us to know who to interact with and what to do is to determine how we feel and what flows for us. I like to say, "The universe has only one way to communicate with us, and that's through people and events." There is no burning bush from which God will speak to us and tell us what to do—although our inner being is a good place to hear divine guidance. If someone stops talking to you or you don't get a job, as long as you have done everything you could, then divine guidance is showing you that it's time to go another way.

Many people blame themselves or other people for the outcomes they experience. They say that it's their fault that they have negative interactions with, say, a boyfriend. They say they should have done more for the relationship, that it ended because of them, that they were too sensitive or too needy. They then vacillate to saying, "But this guy is a player. He wasn't emotionally available. He wasn't good for me." Or they blame themselves for getting sick, saying that they should have known their immune system was down and that they shouldn't have gone out.

Remember that blaming is an activity of the mind-created universe. It takes you away from the facts of what is actually occurring. What is actually occurring is an event, situation, or interaction. You experienced it, you felt a certain way about it, and your body may have felt a sensation in response to it. Your soul saw all of this and is in the process of self-navigating—because that's what it does. You don't need to do anything. You can simply move on to the next moment in time.

CONTEMPLATION: INTERNAL CONFLICT

If you are experiencing stress, discomfort, or unhappiness, check in.

Are you fighting what is? Are you creating inner conflict inside? Can you see that this may be causing you additional suffering?

Hold the situation that's bothering you in your mind, then turn your eyes inward, like you have done before.

Once you feel the pressure between your eyes, with this innate understanding of going inward, say, "I wish it had turned out a different way."

Then, gently guide the energy into your lower belly by breathing gently.

Imagine the energy from your mind or heart moving down your body, like sand in an hourglass, until it lands in your lower belly and settles there.

You will feel a bit of heaviness, like you are taking up some space.

From there, ask, "Is there anything I need to be, do, or have to make this situation better?"

Listen for the answer.

Sometimes you will get guidance in that moment, and sometimes you won't. Either way, stay connected. When there is guidance to be given, your soul will reveal it to you.

CHAPTER 14

INTERNAL GPS AND THE PATH TO ALIGNMENT

Take a look at your journey.

Where are you? Are you struggling? Thriving? Flowing?

Can you recognize when you are connected to your internal universe and when you are disconnected from it?

Can you see that the situation, emotion, or thought you're caught up in may not be the thing that is "taking you out" but rather that your disconnection from your soul is the source of your pain?

❋ ❋ ❋

You may be surprised when you learn that all you need to do is connect to your soul to feel relief and be guided toward your next best step. It really is that simple! The way you know you are on the right path is by the way you feel. You can always feel neutral or better—meaning, relaxed in your body and calm in your mind, no matter the situation.

You may be wondering, "Can I really do this? Live from my soul, truly be myself?"

By this point, you might recognize that these types of thoughts come from the mind-created universe. Yes, asking them was a trick! I want you to realize that, although these are good questions, they are coming from a space that will never give you an answer or allow you to be yourself.

I remember going through this type of questioning. I had forgotten how to be myself. I was disconnected from my soul for so long that being natural wasn't comfortable. I had no idea what it looked or felt like to be myself, and the thought of it was scary. "What if I make a mistake?" I wondered. "I could be doing this all wrong. I might be judged and misunderstood by others." These thoughts hindered my full expression and my ability to live from my soul.

Not living from your soul is a silent death. You feel an emptiness inside, you run around trying different activities to feel better, and you miss the most important key to your fulfillment and happiness: yourself! Your soul is your superpower, the key to living a fulfilled and happy life. Your task is to connect to your soul. Your gauge as to whether you are doing that or not is the way you feel.

When you feel good, you are in alignment, connected to your soul. There is no resistance, and your body, mind, and soul are moving as one unit. When you don't feel good, you are off balance. Some part of you—your mind or your body—is fighting with yourself and your life.

Over time, I developed the following three simple sketches to help you evaluate if you are in alignment or not. Let's go through them together.

This picture depicts you when you are fully in alignment. In other words, your mind, body, and soul are all working together. There is no conflict. You are moving as one unit. This can only happen when you are living from your soul and not fighting what is happening in your life.

More often than you may recognize, your mind is what fights what is happening. Your mind judges yourself and the situation, wanting it to be different. This creates a never-ending loop of thought.

Your body reacts to the situation by tensing up and trying to not feel any emotions or sensations related to what is happening. This can feel extremely uncomfortable. You may experience pain in different parts of your body without realizing it is the resistance that is creating it. Your mind continues this process and takes you even further away from what is happening by thinking incessantly so that you don't feel this discomfort. It does this by analyzing the discomfort and putting it into categories, saying things like, "I am anxious," rather than just feeling it. This keeps moving you further and further away from the emotion of the actual situation.

Your soul is here to experience all of life. It is present with everything that is happening in your life, but you can't connect to it. What is needed is for you to be connected to your soul and allow your body and mind to follow the soul's lead. In order to do this, tune in to yourself. If your body tenses or your mind tries to go somewhere, just watch it. Connect to your core as part of the present moment experience. When you do so, every sensation, thought, emotion, and action will be in the now and from the now. This will keep your soul, body, and mind all here and now.

This is a picture that depicts you when you are here now—because that's actually the only place you can be—but your mind is wandering off somewhere else. You're not aware of the present moment. You're thinking about other things and missing the vibrancy and fullness of life.

This state creates anxiety, depression, and loneliness because thinking about things outside of the present moment disconnects you from your center. Nothing can be done with your thoughts because they are not real. They aren't happening now. Intuitively, your body knows this and feels stress because it can't resolve an illusion; it can only resolve what's right in front of it.

* * *

Take a moment to look around.

Does what you see match what you are thinking?

Is what you are thinking happening *now*?

If it isn't, and you can't respond in this moment to what you are thinking, then you are stuck in a mind-created universe and creating stress in your body. You are out of alignment.

* * *

There is a way to use thoughts to heal and create, but those thoughts are the ones you are choosing. They are grounded in the present moment, so they are in alignment. Thoughts you don't choose are the problematic ones. They drag you into a mind-created universe and a never-ending loop that disconnects you from your soul and your present moment experience.

This is a picture that depicts you when you're so caught up in a past event that you've forgotten where you are altogether. Moving this far away from your center can result in panic attacks and illness. Your body panics because it cannot resolve your upset; you are too far removed from your center. You lack awareness of the present moment—the only place where things can be resolved. In this state, you will do anything to get out of your own skin, pause life, and escape.

This state is what typically triggers addiction. Addiction is a perpetual cycle. It creates a temporary pause or a false reprieve. It is an attempt to feel good through a disconnected method. What you are actually looking for is alignment. You need to come back home to yourself and relax into the core of who you are with no apologies. Who you are is okay with your soul, no matter what your mind or society says.

If you have ever played a sport or exercised, you've heard experts tell you to "engage your core." This is because your movement happens from your core and around your core.

Life is much the same. Connection originates through the belly button and continues through your lower belly and pelvis. This area is where your true self lives. It is your place to plug in and connect to your inner guide. It is the way to access the whole universe and your bliss.

It would make sense that we came to this game called life equipped with the ability to navigate it well and feel good as we do it. In order to do that, we must live from the soul and utilize the tools given.

So how do you do this?

❊ ❊ ❊

Pretend you've been reborn. You are a baby again.

Can you connect to that part of yourself?

Can you feel the joy that lives inside of you—your eyes wide with wonder, observing and taking in the world around you as though you are seeing it for the first time?

You check in with yourself before taking action.

You are flowing with life and moving where you want.

Feel that.

If it feels good, continue. If it doesn't, cry.

This is you in alignment. Throughout the day, check in with yourself to see when you are in alignment and when you are not.

Can you tell the difference? Are you able to reconnect?

❊ ❊ ❊

Your internal GPS system is how you find your way back into alignment. It gives you clues by telling you where your energy is. We explored energy earlier and discussed how it can be either in the head, heart, or center. Knowing where your energy is will explain why you are reacting, ruminating, or relaxed. If you notice that you are out of alignment, you can then decide to take the path back to yourself—not by regulating your nervous system with breathing techniques that make you feel better in the moment, although using them is appropriate when you just need to get through a situation and feel better. Understand that if you want to be truly in alignment, you will need your soul to lead the way. You can't interfere with your self-navigation system by changing the energy superficially. You may end up doing that very same breathing process to regulate your nervous system, but you will do it because it came from your internal guidance, not from a habitual prescription. The outcome will be completely different: it will result in lasting relief rather than temporary relief.

The soul is always alive and alert in the now; it must see and lead you to what is best for you in that moment and that particular situation. Think about the role of a secret shopper. If the staff knew that someone was watching them, they would behave differently, and the company wouldn't get a good gauge of what's really going on. In much the same way, if your mind changes the energy without doing it from an authentic place, then your soul cannot see what's really happening. Your self-navigation system gets interrupted and is unable to do its task.

I have three questions I ask to help me gauge if I am in my internal universe or not:

1. Do I want what I am saying or thinking to be true in my life?

2. Does thinking or saying this feel good?

3. Do I want to keep feeling this way?

If you answer "no" to one or all of these questions, you are in a mind-created universe.

Think of it like driving. If you're planning to go north, but the numbers on the highway mileage signs are getting lower, you're going in the wrong direction. If you keep going this way, you will get further and further from your desired destination. If you are thinking, talking, and dealing with a situation and you feel tension or resistance inside, you're barking up the wrong tree. If you keep going in this direction, you will go deeper and deeper into the mind-created universe. The direction you want to go in is toward your soul. It will help you figure out a solution if there is a problem. It will help you to see clearly. You will be able to feel neutral or better, no matter what the situation is.

I see our self-navigation system as being much like our self-healing system. If I get a cut, it scabs and heals on its own. If something comes up that doesn't serve me, my soul sees it. If I don't interfere with its natural process, it will guide me and keep me headed toward where I want to go and what feels good.

Where I am at this moment in time is my starting point. It is the gauge that shows me how I am doing. Recognizing that I am out of alignment or that my reality is in contradiction to what I want is the first coordinate in my internal GPS system. My destination is alignment. My connection to my soul is the route. All I need to do is allow the soul to see, which I do by observing without trying to make my situation look or feel better. I allow my whole being to be with the present moment just as it is.

This is something most of us were not allowed to do as children. If someone broke my blocks and I got upset, my mom would say, "Don't cry," or "Don't get angry. You will build another one. Here, have some ice cream." This was well-intentioned, but I was sad and angry. What's wrong with that? If I had been allowed to feel that emotion, it would have washed right through me. My soul would have self-navigated through it and passed through it, and no universe would have been created around it. But because the emotion was not allowed to be fully felt or expressed, my mind came in to stop it. My mind created absolutes like, "I won't invite him to play again," or, "I'll break his blocks the next time we play again." Then, it thought about these and other scenarios incessantly. Meanwhile, my body stored the emotion it wasn't allowed to express. Chances are that the next time I was with that friend, or any friend that my mind said might do the same thing, my body reacted even before the friend did anything, simply because I was anticipating him breaking my blocks.

These days, I really honor my reactions, thoughts, and emotions. I don't look at them as anything other than gauges that show me where I am at in this moment. This allows my soul to see what is needed.

You learned to identify your thoughts and emotions earlier in the book, when you identified the "I feel" sentences. This step is crucial, although it's often quite difficult. Many of us have had to hide the truth of what is happening inside of us for years, so we have difficulty identifying it. It's okay if you are not sure what your truth is. Just go with what you know. You will hear yourself saying things to yourself, such as, "I am so anxious, I can't take it." Even if this isn't the full truth, you can use it until you get better at identifying what is really bothering you.

After you've identified your truth, turn your eyes inward and observe the thoughts and emotions connected to your situation without engaging or pushing them away. Once you do this, three things can happen:

1. You feel relief. The feeling or emotion disappears, and you move on. The situation resolves itself without you having to suffer during the process.

2. You get information. Your soul uses that information to provide guidance on how to approach or solve the situation.

3. You decide you want something different in your life. Your soul will show you the way towards creating what you want.

Your soul can create any possibility it wants, so it doesn't worry about a current situation that isn't wanted. It allows the situation to be. By fully being where you are and allowing the situation to be, all aspects of the situation can be revealed—not just the limited parts the mind sees. The soul has the ability to see the situation in its entirety and naturally know what to do.

Should you decide that you want to create something else in your life, you must first decide what it is that you want. This can only happen *after* you have observed your thoughts and emotions and you have come to a neutral state. Otherwise, you will create your new reality from a place of lack and desperation. That place is a product of a mind-created universe, and what you create from there won't necessarily be what you truly want. Instead, it will be a reaction to what you don't want.

Once you have decided what you want—from a grounded place that is connected to your soul and your internal universe—imagine it, and see how much you can feel it. Feeling it is actually more important than imagining it. Every morning and evening, imagine what you want so that your body and mind can become comfortable with the idea. If you find that feeling this new idea is difficult to do, you don't fully believe in what you want. You'll need to keep practicing until it feels natural. If feeling it is easy, then you will naturally move towards your desire using the guidance of your soul.

PRACTICE: IMAGINING CHANGE

What do you want to be different in your life?

How would you know that this difference manifested in your life? What would it look like, feel like?

Can you close your eyes and imagine that this manifestation is happening now?

Once you feel the feeling that you would get when you have what you want, breathe into your lower belly and ask your soul, "What do I need to be, do, or have in this moment to help me move toward what I want?"

Sometimes you will get guidance right away; sometimes you won't. That's okay. Sometimes there is something to do; sometimes there isn't.

Guidance can also be your soul telling you to wait. Just listen and follow.

CHAPTER 15

NAVIGATING INTERPERSONAL INTERACTIONS

Sometimes during interactions, you forget about yourself. This happens when everything you do is in relation to the other person. You take space from the other person, you give space to the other person, and you react to what the other person did and said. In relating this way, your life becomes about some outside force rather than about your internal world.

In healthy interactions, we move from inside toward what is best for our growth and development, and the other person does the same. Each person is on their own separate train going their own way. The two trains interact for a moment that may last anywhere from a split second to many decades. We may visit the other person's train while interacting, but it's important for us to always remember that their train is not our train. We need to go back to our train once the interaction is complete.

During an interaction, you may feel like you are on the other person's train—and perhaps you are. If so, feel free to play on their train! But make sure to always come back to your own train, and make sure that your play is in alignment with your soul. One way to do this is to ask yourself, "Is what I am doing now in my highest and best good?" meaning, "Will it lead me toward what is best for me?" Feel the feeling of connection from inside your body instead of just focusing on the other person. Once you are connected, the answer will be clear.

At times, we have the tendency to do what we think is best for the other person at the expense of what our own soul wants. This is moving from a place of disconnection from our internal universe.

One day, I was working with a client to improve her interactions with her family. She said, "I think I am on my parents' train and in the overhelping universe because I am spending so much time taking care of them."

"Are you doing this at the expense of yourself?" I asked. She said yes. "Well, when you are feeling 'off' in the moment—not while thinking or talking to someone about the situation, but when you are actively involved in helping your parents—do you still think that this is true?"

She paused and checked. Then she said, "No, I know that taking care of them is what I need to be doing right now. I am relaxed inside."

The internal universe is here and now. Discussing, analyzing, and reviewing a situation is the mind's game. We are playing the soul's game. The rules are simple. Right here, right now, how do you feel in your center? If you feel relaxed and grounded, then no matter what you are doing, thinking, or feeling, it is happening from your soul and is authentic to your present moment experience.

Sometimes, people disconnect you from your center without your awareness. It took me a while to recognize the subtlety of how other people can affect me and how their thoughts can latch on to me and disconnect me from my soul. I could be talking to someone with a very strong opinion or belief and suddenly find myself confused or agreeing with them without even knowing why, let alone choosing to do so. It was as though their strong voice and conviction penetrated me, and suddenly, I was reeled in. This created confusion and conflict inside of me, making it difficult to know my own truth. Clearly, I became disconnected from my internal universe.

At one point, I was listening to lots of podcasts and advice from experts who emphasized the importance of meditating and waking up early. So, I started telling myself that I needed to meditate more, do more, and be different—all in the name of being a better person. I invested extra time into meditating, and when I didn't do it, I felt guilty. Imposter syndrome crept in. I thought, "If everyone is telling me that this is what I need to be doing, and I am not doing it, then I must be wrong." As you can imagine, this created a huge amount of discomfort in me! I was beating myself up for not being good enough to fill someone's made-up prescription that was designed to help me reach some made-up destination. The discomfort I felt told me that I was in a should universe, created by someone else's strong beliefs that I latched on to, not my own. These beliefs disconnected me from my truth.

I couldn't follow through on their suggestions because, internally, I didn't want to. This realization brought me great relief. Instead of doing what they were telling me to do, I reconnected to my internal universe and did what I wanted to do. Sometimes, it was listening to a podcast. Sometimes, it was meditating. Sometimes, it was taking a walk. Other times, it was dancing. I continually checked in with my soul and decided what to do. I always knew I was on the right track when I felt at ease and in the flow.

When you are checking to see if you are in the flow, keep in mind that there is a difference between "force" and "intensity." You can be in the flow and be very intense about it because you are getting something done that your soul wants to do. You might even feel a bit of tension as you push through an extra hour of work or exercise a bit longer if, in your core, there is total relaxation and a knowing that what you are doing is right. That would still be considered "ease." Force is what you experience when you feel off, when you feel overwhelmed, when you are about to cry, when your mind is pulling you away from the present and putting you down, when you are dreaming about your addiction, or when you are having anxiety or a panic attack. It might be a powerful sensation, like intensity, but it is a sensation that comes from a place of disconnection.

Life is a moving, breathing, living thing. Each moment is a fresh, new moment. Each day is a fresh, new day. Your ability to see what you need is always available to you.

CHAPTER 16

RESOLVING
INTERNAL DIVISION

As I spent more time in my internal universe, I became more aware of the parts of the day when I was not in it.

For example, I noticed that I had a habit of repeating the same conversation over and over again to myself. Check to see if you do this as well. Can you see that it keeps you from the present moment? I realized this and asked myself, "Is this really necessary?" I wondered. "Is my brain trying to resolve something? Am I unsure about myself? If so, am I repeating this exchange to become clearer?"

The process I do to see what this repetition is all about is always the same. I become aware of my incessant thinking. Then, I turn my eyes inward and notice it while also including everything else that is occurring in my present moment experience. Then, I ask myself, "What information is here for me?

When I went through this process, it helped me realize that I repeated these types of conversations over and over again in my mind in order to change what had occurred during them, to predict future conversations, and/or to justify to myself that what I was doing or thinking was correct. When I recognized what was occurring, I took a breath into my lower belly and checked in with my soul by asking, "Is there anything I want/need to do now to resolve this?" I listened for any guidance and took action or inaction based on that guidance.

But I also found that I replayed conversations even when I wasn't trying to change anything about them. One day, I found myself replaying the same scenario over and over again, and I wanted to get to the bottom of it. I remembered that when I had shared a story with my friend about a date I went on with someone I had just met at a workshop, my friend had given me her unsolicited input. "Be careful," she had said, before starting to give me her thoughts about the potential dangers of dating a "stranger."

"Please don't share this with me," I said. "It's not helpful for me to hear something negative right now."

"But I'm your friend, and as your friend, I need to share this," she replied. Knowing I couldn't stop her from offering her advice, I put the phone on the lowest volume. Then, I put it on the sofa next to me and covered it with towels so I didn't hear what she had to say. I could hear her voice but not her words. I only heard the last three: "Be very careful." I picked up the phone when she was done, said, "Okay," and then changed the subject. I didn't think that conversation had any bearing on me.

But it did.

I was fighting that conversation—both in the moment and after the fact—and the fighting was what was causing me to keep repeating the scenario. I was fighting subconsciously while she was talking with me, which is why I had put the phone down. Then, after the fact, my mind kept replaying what she had told me. This was creating conflict within myself.

I decided to put an end to that conflict and acknowledge what she said as a truth: "Yes, I need to be careful." When I did that, the thoughts stopped.

Stating that possibility, even though it was one I didn't want, removed the internal conflict and allowed my mind to rest. As I stated that truth, a breath came from the inside. It told me that I was moving in the right direction. My soul was no longer blocked by my mind. My mind was quiet, and I felt connected.

What would happen if I did this every time something came up that I was trying to push away for fear of facing it, or not wanting it to be true, not wanting to entertain any negativity? What if I just acknowledged that, yes, I messed up in this situation, and I had no idea what I was doing? Could this simple step quiet my mind and keep me connected to my soul?

I have discovered that it does. Give it a try and see for yourself.

PRACTICE: BEING WITH WHAT IS

What situation keeps replaying in your mind?

What is the discomfort you are trying to avoid feeling by continuously thinking about it?

Acknowledge that, yes, this result is one of the possibilities in life.

Observe the reaction of your mind and body.

Tell your mind that it doesn't need to resolve the situation. Your soul is on it.

Notice what happens inside.

CONCLUSION

Remember that baby? Well, now she is all grown up and wonders if she did life correctly, if she is living her purpose.

Human beings have always struggled with existential questions. We feel like we have to figure out who we are and what our purpose is.

Throughout my life, I have asked myself questions like, "Who am I? What do I believe? What am I here for?" I didn't want to answer them based on what leaders, parents, teachers, or my community had told me. I really wanted to find my own truth.

Then, at some point, I started realizing that these questions were the wrong ones to ask. They are questions of the mind. Their answers will constantly change based on new facts and experiences, things you hear and see, and what others around you say. Answers to these kinds of questions are inevitably based on conditioning and beliefs, such as what we think we're good at and what we've been told by others.

I knew I could not find out who I was using my mind. The answer needed to come from a deeper place—from my soul.

I recognized that I was trying to "think up" an answer instead of allowing the divine—and the answer—to flow through me. It became clear to me that there was only one way for that flow to happen, and that was to be totally in the present and available, not bogged down by my mind with its concepts, ideas, and thoughts. Only by being here, in the moment, could I really see what is in front of me, know what is needed, and move from within.

Who I am has nothing to do with what I do or think. It only has to do with how present I can be in each moment of my life. It has to do with how connected I am to my soul and how willing I am to live each moment of my life—no matter what emotion, personality trait, or event is showing up. It is about not being afraid of life or of myself. Who I am is about living fully as my authentic self in each moment, allowing the divine force to move through me. This makes everything I do divine.

Experimenting with being present and connected to my soul revealed just how little control I had over my thoughts. It also revealed that this lack of control didn't really matter. I was able to feel the warmth that came through me when I was connected. I was able to feel that deep breath that my soul breathed when it felt heard. I was able to know things, intuit things, follow my internal guidance, and flow with life. I put thought in the background, allowing it but not giving it any attention.

In life, we are in one of four places at all times:

1. We're stuck in a universe and busy with that;

2. We're observing and seeing ourselves;

3. We're creating what we want; or

4. We're connected to our soul and living life.

No one of these places is better than the other! It is okay to be wherever you are. We are not here on Earth to try to do anything in particular. We are here to understand ourselves and learn to live life fully and joyfully. Living this way enables us to be fully ourselves, to share our gifts with the world, and to be available to others. Living this way enhances all of our interactions and relationships.

So, if you're stuck in a universe, just acknowledge and understand it. It's a result of your programming, and it's okay. Remember that if you start judging it, you stay stuck. If you observe it and understand it, you are starting to make your way out of it. Observing it will change it. This will open up space for you to reconnect to your soul and live from your internal universe. From there, you can see what it is you want and need to help you create the life you desire.

I want to make something clear: You don't have to be perfect at this! You don't have to do everything right. You just have to be real with yourself so your soul can see clearly. When you are fully present in the moment, willing to be with your truth, and living from your internal universe, any trauma and negative beliefs will be self-navigated by your soul.

How you feel will tell you when you are living from your soul. If you feel relaxed, good, and in the flow, you are in your internal universe. If you don't feel this way, then you are disconnected. Your path to feeling better lies in reconnecting to your soul.

The divine lives in each and every one of us. I call this divine force *the soul.* You may call it source energy, infinite being, inner self, or any other term. Regardless of the name you use, your soul decided to live for this period of time in your unique container. Your task now is to remember this.

My hope is that by sharing my journey and my understanding, I have helped awaken you to your soul to guide you on this beautiful adventure called life.

RESOURCES TO
CONTINUE YOUR JOURNEY

In this book, you've learned the principles behind the MindBrand™ Method. While the ideas are simple, making them a part of your life isn't always easy.

That's why I offer a variety of resources to support you in connecting to the soul.

These include:
- MindBrand™ online courses
- Wellness retreats
- One-on-one coaching and psychotherapy

For more information about all of these, please go to my website.

www.thedebbiegottlieb.com

ABOUT THE AUTHOR

Debbie Gottlieb is a licensed psychotherapist who has diverse international training in psychotherapy and spirituality; certifications in yoga, meditation, and breathwork; and over fourteen years of experience in her private psychotherapy practice. Debbie specializes in individual counseling for stress and anxiety relief, depression, couples counseling, and more. Debbie created the MindBrand Method™, a practical and accessible method to connect to the soul and live a fulfilled and authentic life. She guides her clients in applying this method through private counseling, online programs, and retreats. Debbie has been a seeker of inner truth since she can remember; she read her first self-help book when she was eight years old. Her journey led her to a discovery of the soul, the most freeing and transformative experience of her life. Debbie has a passion for salsa dancing, family, hiking, and yoga. The Fort Lauderdale Award Program named her the Best Psychotherapist in Fort Lauderdale, Florida in 2022 and 2023.